Scenic Driving

GEORGIA

Donald W. Pfitzer
&
LeRoy Powell

FALCON™

HELENA, MONTANA

*A*FALCONGUIDE

Falcon Press is continually expanding its list of recreational guidebooks. All books include detailed descriptions, accurate maps, and all the information necessary for enjoyable trips. You can order extra copies of this book and get information and prices for other Falcon guidebooks by writing Falcon Press, P.O. Box 1718, Helena, MT 59624 or calling toll-free 1-800-582-2665. Also, please ask for a free copy of our current catalog.

Cover photo: Azalea Drive, Callaway Gardens, by Donald W. Pfitzer.
Back cover photo: Male wood duck, by Donald W. Pfitzer.

All black and white photos by the authors.
All photos in color section by Craig M. Tanner.

Library of Congress Cataloging-in-Publication Data

Pfitzer, Donald W.
   Scenic driving Georgia / Donald W. Pfitzer & LeRoy Powell.
      p.   cm.
   ISBN 1-56044-411-8 (pbk.)
   1. Georgia—Guidebooks.   2. Automobile travel—Georgia-
-Guidebooks.   I. Powell, LeRoy, 1943- .   II. Title.
F284.3.P47 1996
917.5804'43—dc20   96-2544
                                                                    CIP

Contents

Acknowledgments

In preparing a work like this there are many people who contribute to its completion. It is not possible to acknowledge them all, however, there are a few who have been exceptionally helpful. We would like to thank all the people of the Department of Natural Resources who provided information and help, especially Commissioner Lonice Barrett, Harvey Young, and the several state park managers who gave of their time and expertise.

Thanks are due David Waller, Director, and Dottie Head, Public Affairs Coordinator of the Wildlife Resources Division, who were most helpful in providing information and helping with arrangements on several drives. Darrell Watson and Jim Gillis of Grand Bay Wildlife Management Area helped as guides and with information on this new state area. Changes in highway designations, new and rerouted roads were frequently a problem in designing drives. Jerry Stargell, Department of Transportation, was most helpful in overcoming this problem.

Keith O. Wooster, Wildlife Biologist with USDA Forest Service at Chatsworth provided suggestions and useful information on the habitat and road condition advice on the Cohutta drive. Kathryn W. Tilley provided particularly useful information and assistance at Callaway Gardens.

Two very special people, Valeria Powell and Billie Pfitzer, were particularly helpful with encouragement, riding shotgun on many drives, and they spent many hours reading manuscripts and offering constructive suggestions.

Locator Map

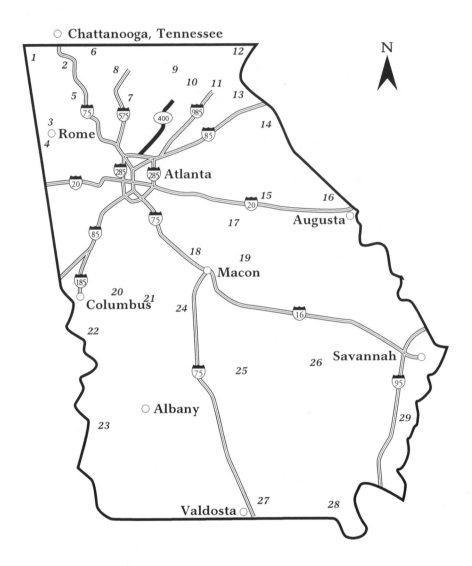

Map Legend

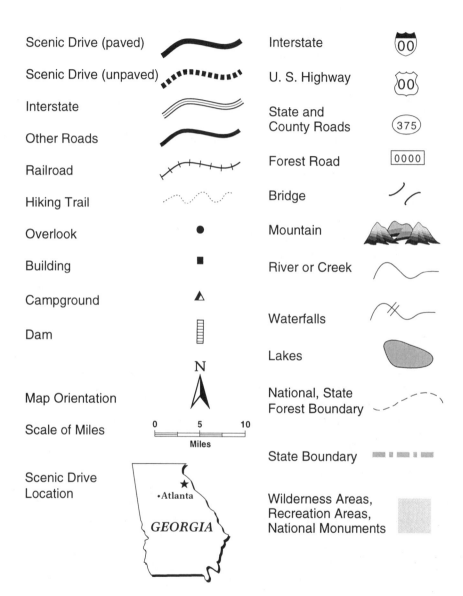

Scenic Drive (paved)

Scenic Drive (unpaved)

Interstate

Other Roads

Railroad

Hiking Trail

Overlook

Building

Campground

Dam

Map Orientation

Scale of Miles

Scenic Drive
Location

Interstate

U. S. Highway

State and
County Roads

Forest Road

Bridge

Mountain

River or Creek

Waterfalls

Lakes

National, State
Forest Boundary

State Boundary

Wilderness Areas,
Recreation Areas,
National Monuments

N

0   5   10
Miles

★
•Atlanta

GEORGIA

Introduction

From the Atlantic Ocean, coastal barrier islands, and great expanses of salt marsh to the southern Appalachian Mountains, Georgia's natural beauty spans five physiographic provinces and more than 300 miles from south to north. Five interstate highways with spurs crisscross the state with 1,200 miles of limited-access driving. These superhighways provide easy access to byways promising many miles of interesting and pleasant driving for the seeker of scenic adventure.

Of the more than 2,000 miles and twenty-nine drives covered in this guide, only about 50 miles are on unpaved roads. Some are on wide divided highways, but most are on secondary roads. The drives were selected to include scenic, historic, and unique areas in all parts of the state.

Georgia is the largest state east of the Mississippi River and contains a great range of habitats. The drives discussed in this guide cover all physiographic provinces and most of the diversity found in each.

From south to north, the first and most diverse province is the Coastal Plain. It can generally be divided into the lower and upper sections. The lower Coastal Plain includes the coastal islands as well as salt marshes influenced by marine tides and the extensive area of flat longleaf pine forests and wiregrass. North of this, in the upper Coastal Plain, are broadleaf forests and more rolling topography. This area includes a wide range of habitats and supports orchards of peaches and pecans. It is also the area of extensive peanut, cotton, soybean, and tobacco farms. Rivers running through these sections of the state are generally flat and slow moving.

The Fall Line is the northernmost section of the Coastal Plain, crossing the state in an undulating band from Columbus to Augusta. Ridges and mixed hardwood-pine forest characterize this region. This is an area of fast-moving streams, some with waterfalls. Early settlers established water-powered factories on the rapids and falls. Many road cuts show the red clay subsoil.

The Piedmont Province is a broad band between the Fall Line and the Mountains. At the turn of the last century this area was agriculturally productive. Soils wore out from overuse, and the farms were abandoned because they could not support the families living there. Today those small farms have become consolidated into larger farms of pasture and pine land. Many dairies are in the lower Piedmont. Extensive pine plantations produce many tons of pulpwood to drive paper mills. The upper Piedmont, with its steep ridges and narrow valleys, lies against the Blue Ridge and Ridge and Valley provinces. At one time the Piedmont was a massive and beautiful hardwood forest with openings resulting from fires and granite outcrops. One of the latter, Stone Mountain near Atlanta, is the largest such

Old-fashioned rose at Thomasville, Georgia, "The City of Roses."

outcropping, or monadnock, in the world. These unique geologic features are scattered across the lower Piedmont.

The Blue Ridge physiographic province encompasses the mountains of the north and northeast corner of the state. These mountains are among the oldest in the world. Although the highest points are only in the 4,500-foot range, they are high enough to retain some of the plants and animals characteristic of northern, or boreal, forests. The softly rounded mountains may not be as dramatic as the Rockies but they have a beauty and intimacy all their own. Several of the drives are in this area.

The Ridge and Valley and Cumberland Plateau provinces are in the northwest corner and have some of the boldest and most dramatic mountains, cliffs, and ravines in the state. Cloudland Canyon State Park, Lookout Mountain, Berry College, and much Civil War history are in these two areas.

Throughout the state, Georgia's State Parks and Historic Sites Division manages fifty-eight widely diverse units, from the Atlantic Coast and the Okefenokee Swamp in south Georgia to Cloudland Canyon in the northwest corner and to Black Rock Mountain near Clayton. Several parks are included or are in close proximity to the drives. A ParkPass is required for parked vehicles in all state parks. A daily ($2) or annual ($25) ParkPass is available and is valid at all state parks. The daily ParkPass is valid at all state parks visited the same day. Wednesdays are free days for day-use visitors. For campsite and lodge reservations at all state parks you can call (770) 389-7275 or (800) 864-7275.

There are ten national parks, monuments, and recreation areas managed by the National Park Service in Georgia. They range from Cumberland Island National Seashore on the southeast corner to Chickamauga and Chattanooga National Military Park in the northwest corner of the state. Two drives in this book feature Ocmulgee National Monument near Macon and Andersonville National Historic Site near Americus.

Georgia has two national forests that include over 800,000 acres. The largest is the 750,000-acre Chattahoochee National Forest that encompasses much of the North Georgia mountains. Oconee National Forest is in the Piedmont region and covers more than 108,000 acres. In these forest areas you will find many miles of unpaved Forest Service roads that lead into backcountry areas. These roads are numbered; with a Forest Service map, they are relatively easy to follow and explore. Only a few of these roads are included in the scenic drives. The rest are left for the adventurous souls who want to take side trips off the described drive. Excellent maps of the forest and wilderness areas are available from the USDA Forest Service district offices listed in the appendix for any drive that passes through a part of the Chattahoochee or Oconee forests.

Eleven National Wildlife Refuges with more than 450,000 acres are managed by the U.S. Fish and Wildlife Service in Georgia. The largest and most well known encompasses virtually all the Okefenokee Swamp. One of the drives in this book goes completely around the swamp. Along the Atlantic Coast is the Savannah National Wildlife Refuge complex, where coastal marsh and island areas are dedicated to migratory waterfowl and other wildlife for wildlife watching, fishing, hunting, hiking, and photography. The principal refuges in this complex are Savannah Refuge on the South Carolina–Georgia line, Wassaw, Harris Neck, and Blackbeard south of Savannah. Only Savannah and Harris Neck refuges are accessible by car. Piedmont National Wildlife Refuge is in the rolling topography of the Piedmont region and is included in one of the drives.

The Georgia Wildlife Resources Division manages seventy-eight Wildlife Management Areas that collectively include a million acres. They are located in all regions of the state, with the greatest number in the northern half. The drives pass through or brush against many of these areas of unique wildlife habitat. These areas are good places for birding and other wildlife watching and many days of hunting and fishing.

The diversity of habitat types supports a wide range of plant and animal species. There are more than 150 species of trees and more than a thousand kinds of shrubs, vines, flowering herbaceous plants, ferns, mosses, liverworts, lichens, and mushrooms and other fungi. There are 65 species of mammals, 112 species of snakes, lizards, and turtles, and 83 kinds of salamanders, toads, and frogs.

Georgia is steeped in Revolutionary War and Civil War history. Civil War buffs will find points of interest throughout the state. Revolutionary War historic sites are mainly along the coast.

Throughout Georgia, one may easily feel the historical influence of American Indians. Because many of the roads in Georgia were originally constructed on historic Indian routes, some drives in this book follow or cross these trails.

Several drives reflect on the early plantation life that was so much a part of Georgia's past.

There are few natural lakes in Georgia. However, the state has dozens of hydroelectric power dams and reservoirs. Drives such as the one around Carters Lake in north Georgia attest to the scenic value of some of these impoundments. They range in size from a few hundred acres to more than 55,000 acres and are important recreational resources. Additionally, thousands of small farm ponds and water storage lakes are scattered in all parts of the state.

There are many interesting and scenic places in and close to the Atlanta metropolitan area. Because of the great changes that are taking place in the road system at the time of this writing, Stone Mountain, the Chattahoochee River on the north side of the city, Kennesaw Mountain National Battlefield Park, Sweetwater Creek State Park, and several others are not included in this guide. Any set of directions would be outdated in only a few months. Drivers who want to explore the Atlanta area should get directions locally.

The drives in *Scenic Driving Georgia* are described from a starting point to an end, or from the starting point through a loop back to the starting point. These routes cross or connect with many other primary and secondary roads, which makes it possible to reach the drives from points other than the starting point. Therefore, you can design your drive to begin wherever it is most convenient for you. A few of the drives are long and could be broken into a two-day drive with camping or other lodging along the way.

The appendix lists the names, addresses, and phone numbers of local visitor information centers, state parks, museums, and the like, and is numerically organized by drive.

For those interested in more detailed discussions of the great environmental diversity in the state, the following books are suggested reading:

Natural Environments of Georgia, by Dr. Charles H. Wharton. Published in 1978 by the Department of Natural Resources, Environmental Protection Division, and the Georgia Geologic Survey, this book is a scholarly treatment of the wide variety of habitats in the state.

Georgia Conservancy's Guide to the North Georgia Mountains. First published in 1990 by the Georgia Conservancy, this guide is on sale at most bookstores and gift shops at state parks.

Georgia Historical Markers, published by Bay Tree Grove, Helen, Georgia 30545. This is a complete text of 1,752 markers erected by theGeorgia Historical Commission along roadways of the state.

Drive 1: Look Up, Look Down, Lookout Mountain Loop

LaFayette to Lookout Mountain

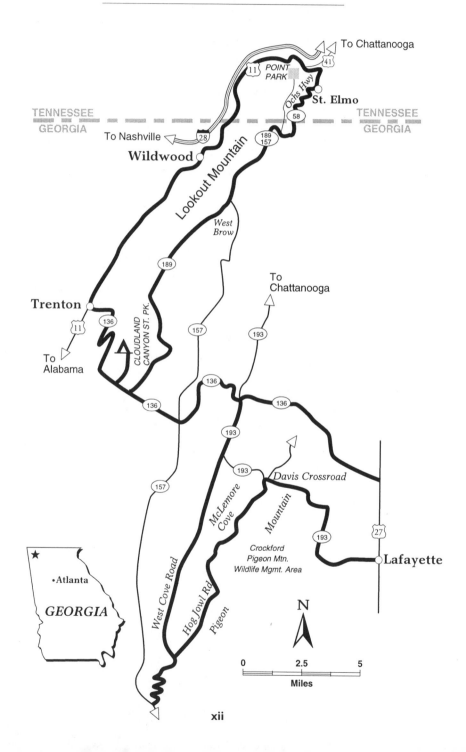

1

Look Up, Look Down, Lookout Mountain Loop

LaFayette to Lookout Mountain

General description: This 128-mile loop drive takes you into the very northwest corner of the state into the Cumberland Plateau's sandstone bluffs and wide valleys. From LaFayette, at the western edge of the Ridge and Valley region, you quickly get sight of Pigeon Mountain, a spur of Lookout Mountain. After rounding the toe of Pigeon Mountain you enter McLemore Cove. From the loop into the cove you climb the eastern escarpment of Lookout Mountain, then continue to Cloudland Canyon State Park. The drive descends the western side of the mountain and goes into the valley, around the north end of Lookout Mountain, and to the edge of Chattanooga. Here you dip into and out of Tennessee very quickly. Back up Lookout Mountain you can visit Rock City Garden, Point Park, and other attractions before going back south on the mountain and into the Chickamauga Valley to close the loop back at LaFayette.

Special attractions: Grand views from the valleys and mountains, the unique McLemore Cove with beautiful farms and views, and the Cumberland Plateau's southern limits, which rise 2,000 feet above the valley floor. Cloudland Canyon State Park, Point Park, and Rock City Gardens are on Lookout Mountain.

Location: Northwest corner of the state.

Drive route numbers: Georgia Highways 193 and 136, Georgia Highway 58/U.S. Highway 11, Tennessee Highway 58, Georgia Highways 157 and 189, Hog Jowl Road, and West Cove Road.

Travel season: A year-round drive with emphasis on spring wildflowers and flowering trees and fall leaf color. Weather is usually cooler on the mountains in summer, and there is a possibility of snow in winter.

Camping: Cloudland Canyon has tent and RV campsites and cabins. There is primitive camping in the nearby Armuchee District of Chattahoochee National Forest.

Services: Motels and restaurants in LaFayette and in Chattanooga, Tennessee.

Nearby attractions: Chattahoochee National Forest, Armuchee District; Crockford-Pigeon Mountain Wildlife Management Area; Chickamauga-Chattanooga National Military Park; and the Tennessee Aquarium, Battles of Chattanooga Museum and many other activities in Chattanooga, Tennessee.

 # The drive

This loop drive starts at LaFayette, in the Ridge and Valley physiographic province of northwest Georgia, and leads onto the Cumberland Plateau, then goes north to Chattanooga, Tennessee, before coming back along the crest of Lookout Mountain, to the starting point. Travelers who want to take their time would do well to plan to drive it in two days, stopping overnight at Cloudland Canyon State Park or in Chattanooga.

You'll get the view from the valley up and from the mountain down. One portion of the drive that cannot be missed is McLemore Cove, a beautiful valley ringed on three sides by steep, forested slopes. The entire drive is particularly scenic during the spring, when the trees display a palette of pastel greens and the dogwoods and wild azaleas are in bloom, and in the fall, when the foliage is painted in reds and yellows.

The drive begins in LaFayette, one of two dozen towns in the United States named for the Marquis de LaFayette, hero of the American Revolution. Local pronunciation of the name is "la-FAY-it." Begin at the intersection of U.S. Highway 27 and GA 193, traveling west on GA 193 through the town.

In about 0.5 mile, still following GA 193, you leave the town and enter open countryside. Soon you will see a mountain looming to your left. This is Pigeon Mountain, named for the flocks of now-extinct passenger pigeons that once roosted here by the millions. Much of the mountain is now part of Crockford–Pigeon Mountain Wildlife Management Area, providing hunting as well as camping and hiking trails. About 7 miles from LaFayette is Estelle Camping Area, part of the WMA, used mainly by hunters venturing after deer, turkey, and other wild game on this state-run wildlife management area. This mountain also contains Ellison's Cave, one of the deepest in the world.

About 2 miles later, turn left on Hog Jowl Road. The intersection is called Davis Crossroads, and we are taking a 27-mile side trip into McLemore Cove. You don't have to go, but you'll be glad if you do.

If you like pastoral scenery, this is your place: a broad valley enclosed on three sides by wooded ridges. It is simply beautiful. Hog Jowl Road runs for about 10 miles, where it joins West Cove Road. Turn left and you soon encounter Mountain Cove Farm, where the road is lined on either side by large maple trees, with wide, well-tended pastures just beyond. This, obviously, is a prosperous farming operation. To the left, a paved aircraft runway parallels the road. To the right are neat farmhouses and buildings.

At the back of the cove, the road winds up the ridge. About halfway, there is a good view of McLemore Cove to your left. Continue to wind up the mountain, then turn around when you reach Daugherty Gap, which is

Rock City Gardens, Lookout Mountain.

one of the entrances to Crockford-Pigeon Mountain WMA, on your left.

Going back, continue straight on West Cove Rd., to GA 193, where you turn left. In about 3 miles, you turn left on GA 136, heading west. The road soon begins to rise as you climb the eastern escarpment of Lookout Mountain. Around here, they don't call it an escarpment; here it's called a brow. It's easy to see why, since the steep mountainside resembles a person's forehead. As you climb, the rock outcroppings on the side of the road are limestone, and higher, sandstone. Where you have limestone, you often have caves, and this part of the country has a great many, created as water dissolved limestone and formed cavities in the rock. Lookout Mountain is the beginning of the Cumberland Plateau physiographic province.

To your left, you can see back to McLemore Cove, which you just left, and farther on the horizon, Pigeon Mountain.

As you cross Lookout Mountain, you enter Dade County. This northwesternmost county in Georgia is largely cut off from the rest of the state by the mountain. Being isolated as they are, people around here have an independent way of looking at things. The county is called "The State of Dade," and legend has it that in 1861, Dade County seceded from the Union before the rest of of Georgia did. The county didn't officially return to the United States until July 4, 1945.

About 4 miles past the intersection with GA 189 is the entrance to Cloudland Canyon State Park. It is about 1.5 miles to the parking lot at the canyon rim. This is a good picnic spot with a spectacular view of the gorge formed by Sitton Gulch Creek. A hiking trail leads into the canyon from here.

As you rejoin GA 136, heading west, you soon reach the top edge of the western brow of Lookout Mountain, and a panoramic view westward toward Alabama's Sand Mountain. It is about a 3.5-mile trip to the foot of the mountain. Here, you turn right, picking up U.S. Highway 11 at Trenton. Continue on US 11 (and GA 58) as GA 136 goes to the left. As you travel north, the long western escarpment of Lookout Mountain looms on the right. At this end, the mountain is only a few miles wide at the most, but it is about 50 miles long, running from Chattanooga, Tennessee, into Alabama near Lake Weiss.

Twenty miles from Trenton, just before the Tennessee state line, is a historic marker near the home of Chief Wauhatchee, who led a contingent of Cherokees under Andrew Jackson in the War of 1812. Sadly, he probably was "rewarded" by being herded west with the rest of his people along the Trail of Tears in 1838.

Three miles past the Tennessee line, as you parallel Interstate 24, pick up US 41. What you are doing here is going around the northeast end or "toe" of Lookout Mountain. The river at this point is the Moccasin Bend of the Tennessee River. A little over a mile later, turn left through a railroad underpass, then right under another, and pick up Tennessee Highway 17. This road soon picks up TN 58 at the incline railway station (on the right). A tram here takes passengers straight up the side of the mountain. Seats on the tram car are tilted so the passengers sit level even though the car is tilting at an acute angle. Stay on TN 58, also known as the Ochs Highway. It is named after Adolph S. Ochs, who founded the *Times*, a Chattanooga newspaper, before he moved to New York to found a paper of the same name there.

On your right as you travel up the mountainside, is Ochs Highway Extension. This road will lead you to Point Park, a unit of Chickamauga and Chattanooga National Military Park. Continue straight on Ochs Highway, and cross back into Georgia at the Lookout Mountain city limits. The road becomes GA 157. To the left is the road to Rock City, one of America's best-known roadside attractions. Lured by "See Rock City" signs painted on barn roofs, generations of families have detoured here to visit the trails and attractions of this park set among crevices and boulders on the sandstone cliffs of Lookout Mountain.

Sitton Gulf, Cloudland Canyon State Park.

Continue on GA 157, picking up GA 189, onto the Lookout Mountain Parkway. In less than a mile, you come to Covenant College, a Presbyterian-affiliated school sitting atop the west brow of the mountain. Its main building was originally the famous Lookout Mountain Hotel, but is now owned by the school. The mountaintop here is only a few hundred yards wide, giving you a continuing opportunity to see into the distance. To the east are the peaks of the Great Smoky Mountains.

Continue straight on GA 189 when GA 157 turns off to the left. In about 2.5 miles, there is a scenic overlook, an opportunity to stop and look to the west, at the highway you traveled a few minutes ago, and farther, into Alabama.

Just past the overlook, you come to Lookout Mountain Flight Park, a center for hang-gliders, where adventurers soar off the brow into the west wind. They have tandem hang-gliders with experienced pilots in case you want to see what it's like to jump off a perfectly good mountain on a kite.

Lookout Mountain Parkway snakes its way through the woods atop the mountain, among the shortleaf and white pines, oaks and other hardwoods, and (in the springtime) among the blossoming dogwoods. Because Lookout Mountain's top is a plateau, traveling on the mountaintop gives you only occasional views into the distance; in the valley you always have the scenic vista of mountains around you. And thus, pondering this irony of life, 6 miles past Lookout Mountain Flight Park, turn left on GA 136 and go down the eastern escarpment the way you came up.

Follow GA 136 for the next 20 miles north of Pigeon Mountain to pick up US 27, which takes you back to your starting point.

2

Civil War History

Rocky Face, Fort Oglethorpe, and Chattanooga

General description: This is a 50-mile drive through the Ridge and Valley area in the northwest corner of the state. It begins at Rocky Face and leads to Tunnel Hill, Chickamauga, Missionary Ridge, and Chattanooga. Follow U.S. Highway 41, which has been bypassed by Interstate 75. For the most part, this is a two-lane highway reminiscent of the days before interstates. Short side trips take you to Tunnel Hill tunnels and one of Sherman's headquarters, Chickamauga–Chattanooga National Military Park, the old town of Chickamauga, and along the crest of Missionary Ridge overlooking Chattanooga.

Special attractions: Dalton carpet manufacturing; scenic ridges and mountains; Civil War history on the grounds of actual battles; an excellent visitor information center at the national military park with an outstanding collection of old guns; and fall colors.

Location: Northwest Georgia.

Drive route numbers: I-75, U.S. Highways 41 and 27, Georgia Highways 1 and 2, and a number of named roads for side trips.

Travel season: A year-round drive. Spring and fall are the most comfortable times; spring flowering trees and shrubs are abundant in the woodlands along the way, and fall leaf color is spectacular in the deciduous forest.

Camping: No available camping sites on state or national lands nearby.

Services: The popular chain hotels and motels are at Dalton, Fort Oglethorpe, and Chattanooga. Good restaurants are all along the way. Bed and breakfast at Gordon–Lee Mansion in Chickamauga.

Nearby attractions: Dalton carpet manufacturing; Tennessee Aquarium, Lookout Mountain, and Chickamauga Lake and Dam in Chattanooga; Fort Mountain State Park; Vann House; Crown Gardens and Archives, a center for local history and bedspread tufting that led to the carpet industry; and Praters Mill Country Fair in Dalton in May and October.

 The drive

This drive takes you from Dalton, Georgia, to Chattanooga, Tennessee, with an intimate look at Civil War history. The route includes sites of some of the most famous actions in the northwest Georgia area, including the Great Locomotive Chase of 1862, the battles of Chickamauga and Missionary Ridge of 1863, and Sherman's Atlanta Campaign of 1864. The entire route is never more than 20 miles from an interstate highway, beginning at I-75 and ending at I-24, so lodging, meals, and facilities are always nearby in this highly traveled transportation corridor. Chattanooga offers a host of attractions, and Dalton is a mecca for people shopping for carpets and floor coverings. The city of Dalton advertises itself as "The Carpet Capital of the World," with good reason. In the 1920s, local people became involved in a cottage industry making chenille bedspreads and bathrobes in their mountain cabins. With refining, the same process that produced gaudy peacock- and flower-design bed coverings came to be used in the production of carpeting. You do not have to look far to see how successful the carpet business has become. Outlet stores line the highways for miles around, where you can buy practically any floor covering that exists at a discount price.

This route is also near several other drives, including Drives 1, 5, and 6.

The drive begins at Exit 137 of I-75, just north of Dalton. Go north on US 41/76. That this is a factory area with lots of traffic is soon apparent. Before the interstate highway opened, this road was a main artery between the Midwest and Georgia, and traffic still funnels through the mountain passes at Rocky Face and Tunnel Hill much as it has done since the first settlers arrived and when Union and Confederate armies maneuvered here during the Civil War. Then, even more than now, the lay of the land dictated corridors of travel. Indian trails, pioneer roads, and railroads follow valleys in this section of prominent ridges. The Western & Atlantic Railroad between Atlanta and Chattanooga offered fast transport of troops and materials to Confederate forces, and Union forces wanted to cripple this supply line. First, Andrews' Raiders, then the army under General William Tecumseh Sherman, made it their target.

About a mile past Mill Creek Gap, the road picks up Georgia Highway 201. Continue straight. On your left, GA 201 goes south toward Villanow. This northwest part of the state is marked by ridges and valleys that run northeast to southwest, and most of the main roads follow the valley floors. Roads that go across the ridges generally do so at gaps, such as the one you are in now.

Two miles later, you enter Tunnel Hill. This town is named for the Western & Atlantic Railroad tunnel dug in 1847 through Chetoogeta Mountain, on your right. Today there are two tunnels through the mountain. A newer tunnel, dug in 1928, carries modern rail traffic. To get a better view of the tunnels, turn right just over the railroad bridge on Jordan Street. Then bear right on Oak Street. Cross the railroad tracks, and on the left are several historic markers. Turn left on Clisby Austin Road, on which there is a small covered bridge of recent construction. It has 10 feet of clearance, for those of you with higher vehicles. You may park where the road turns left.

Drive 2: Civil War History
Rocky Face to Fort Oglethorpe to Chattanooga

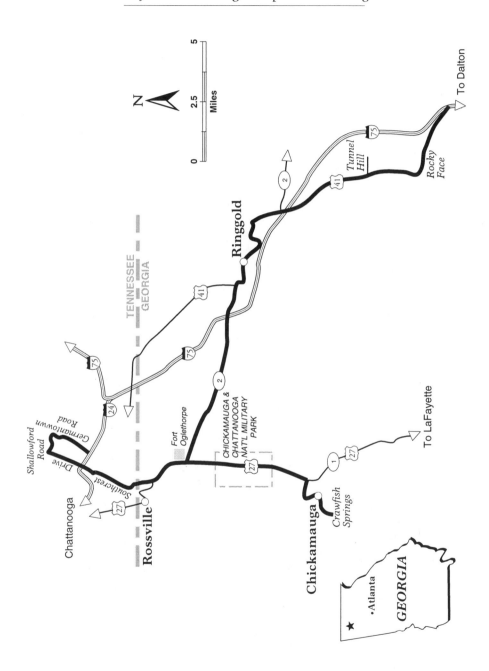

On the right is the Clisby Austin House, which was the headquarters for General Sherman in May 1864. Here, he planned the first moves of his Atlanta Campaign.

On the left is the railroad leading to the two railroad tunnels. The tunnel on the right is the original one, 1,477 feet long. Built in 1848 for the Western & Atlantic Railroad, this line from Chattanooga to Atlanta was the first rail connection from the Atlantic to the Mississippi River valley. It was also the lifeline for men and supplies during the Civil War. In 1862, The Great Locomotive Chase passed through the tunnel, as Union raiders led by James J. Andrews stole the *General*, a Confederate locomotive, in Kennesaw and headed north, intending to destroy tracks and bridges along their way. They were pursued and finally caught by railroad workers in another steam engine, the *Texas*. The tunnel on the left is still in use by CSX Railroad. Both tunnels are on railroad property, and at this writing, visitors are not allowed access to them. The local historical society, however is in negotiations with CSX to allow entry to the old one. Land near the Clisby Austin house is the site of annual Civil War reenactments in the late summer.

Four miles north on US 41, you pass under I-75. A mile later, where the road joins Georgia Highway 2 at Tiger Creek, is the path of an even older route, Old Federal Road. Originally an Indian trading path to Augusta, it opened as a postal route through the Cherokee Nation in 1805. The Old Stone Presbyterian Church here served as a field hospital during the Civil War. Bloodstains are still visible on the wooden floors. The road soon begins to parallel Chickamauga Creek to your left. Across the creek, you can see the tremendous cut blasted in the side of Taylor Ridge to accommodate I-75.

Continue through Ringgold Gap into the town of Ringgold. Its depot, open since 1850, is to the right, above you at the railroad underpass. Its 14-inch-thick sandstone walls were damaged by federal artillery in 1863. You can see where limestone blocks were used to repair the wreckage. A mile and a half past the railroad tracks, turn left on GA 2. Soon you're back to Interstate 75 again, where GA 2 becomes a four-lane highway lined with shopping facilities 7.5 miles to Fort Oglethorpe. A mile or so past the interstate is a view across the valley to Lookout Mountain. Since this is about the only scenic feature of this stretch of highway, enjoy it while you can.

At Fort Oglethorpe, turn left on U.S. Highway 27 and Georgia Highway 1, heading south. This, like US 41, was a major traffic artery from the Midwest to the South and is still busy with mostly local traffic. It goes directly through Chickamauga Battlefield Park, but a bypass around the park is being built, which should help the local traffic and make visiting the park a more pleasant experience.

In a mile you enter the park. Established in 1890, this is the first and largest national military park. On the right, the visitor center and museum

Chattanooga–Chickamauga Battlefield National Military Park. Snodgrass cabin was used as a hospital for both Union and Confederate wounded at the same time.

features interpretive displays about the battle of Chickamauga and a 355-piece collection of military firearms. At the visitor center you can get instructions for driving, hiking, and bicycling tours through the 8,000-acre park and information about the 1,400 monuments and historic markers here. This place is not good for a hit-and-run visit. It is large, spread out, and beautiful, and there's no way you can fully appreciate it in a short visit. Give yourself several hours to roam the grounds.

As you drive south on US 41, there are numerous monuments, markers, and displays commemorating the two-day Civil War battle in September 1863 in which the two sides collectively had over 34,000 killed, wounded, or missing.

Near the visitor center north of the park, the Sixth Cavalry Museum of Fort Oglethorpe is a collection of cavalry equipment and records. South of the park, Lee-Gordon Mill Road is a tree-lined road leading to the town of Chickamauga. Places to visit here include the Gordon-Lee Mansion, which served as a hospital for Union wounded during the battle, and Crawfish Springs, where subterranean water bubbles out of the limestone rock into a large pool.

North of the park, US 27 leads to Rossville, named for Cherokee Chief John Ross. His 1792 log home is here and open for tours from June through September.

Turn right at the Rossville city limit sign on South Crest Road. This small, two-lane, residential street takes you into Tennessee. The state line is about 0.5 mile up the road but is not marked. You will know you are there because Chattanooga and East Ridge city limits signs are at the intersection with John Ross Road. South Crest Rd. runs along the crest of Missionary Ridge, overlooking Chattanooga. On November 25, 1863, Union soldiers acting without orders captured this ridge by charging up its steep sides. There are numerous historical markers regarding the Battle of Missionary Ridge, but the road is too narrow and winding for you to park and inspect them conveniently.

At Crest Road, Bragg's Park has a small parking area with displays about the Chattanooga campaign. The park is named for Braxton Bragg, the Confederate general who lost the battle here partly because he placed his artillery at the top of the ridge, where his cannon could not be depressed enough to fire down at the Union soldiers climbing up towards his position.

Just past Bragg's Park, South Crest Rd. turns left and takes you on a high bridge over I-24. To your left from the bridge, you get a panoramic view of Chattanooga and environs, and to the right, you can look back into Georgia. Just past the bridge is a house with two cannons in the front yard, pointed at the house.

A mile past this strange sight, turn right on Shallowford Road, which will take you down the northeast slope of the ridge. Then turn right on Tunnel Boulevard, bear left on Germantown Road, and follow Germantown Rd. for 2 miles to a left turn onto the access road that takes you to the entrance ramp of I-24. Get on I-24, which leads you to I-75 south, back to Georgia.

Crawfish Springs, town of Chickamauga.

3

Rome and Berry College to Villanow Loop

Johns Mountain and The Pocket

General description: This loop drive covers about 100 miles of hard-surfaced roads through the Ridge and Valley region of northwest Georgia. Taylor Ridge, Johns Mountain, and other ridges provide scenic contrast to the wide pastoral valleys. This drive is rich in human and natural history with abundant spring and summer flowers and fall leaf color.

Special attractions: This drive features attractive valley farms and forested hills. Berry College campus, covering over 27,000 acres, is the largest campus in the country. The buildings are spectacular and the well-kept grounds can be a riot of leaf color in the fall. The campus is a wildlife management area with abundant wildlife frequently visible from the road. Chattahoochee National Forest, Armuchee District, has hiking trails, camping, and grand fall colors and wildflowers; and Johns Mountain Wildlife Management Area and Arrowhead Public Fishing Area both have hiking trails and excellent wildlife watching opportunities.

Location: Northwest Georgia.

Drive route numbers: Interstate 75; Georgia Highway 20; U.S. Highways 41 and 27; and Georgia Highways 1, 201, 136, and 156. Pocket Road, Everett Springs Road, and Lovers Lane are county roads you will travel.

Travel season: Year-round with spring wildflowers and fall leaf color.

Camping: In the Pocket Recreation Area, plus primitive camping in some areas of the national forest.

Services: Motels and restaurants are available in Rome or north of the drive in Summerville.

Nearby attractions: Red Top Mountain State Park; New Echota State Historic Site; Etowah Indian Mounds; Weiss Lake; James H. Floyd State Park; and various Civil War battlegrounds, including Chickamauga-Chattanooga National Military Park, Resaca, Rocky Face, Tunnel Hill, Dalton, and others.

 The drive

The Ridge and Valley region of northwest Georgia is a series of ridges, some called mountains, that lie in a northeast to southwest pattern. Between the prominent ridges are broad agricultural valleys. Rome is near the southern end of this physiographic province that extends into southwest Virginia. Roads follow the valley floors and only occasionally cross over the ridges for grand views of the region. At Rome the Oostanaula and Etowah rivers join to form the Coosa River, which is impounded to become Weiss Lake in Alabama.

The drive begins on the north side of Rome, where GA 1 Loop meets US 27. This is Martha Berry Boulevard. Travel north on US 27/GA 1 for about a mile to the main entrance to the Berry College campus. Turn left into the campus on the wide drive. Pass a small gate building where information and a page-sized map of the campus can be obtained. This entrance road ends at Hermann Hall, the college administration building. A turn to the right takes you to the beautiful Ford Buildings. From here there are a number of possibilities for seeing the campus. It is suggested that you go to the Swan Lake and Frost Memorial Chapel area and to the Old Mill Wheel. On the way there are large wooded areas, all part of the Berry College Wildlife Management Area. The drive around this large campus can be several miles and has not been counted into the total miles for the main drive.

Across the highway from the campus entrance is the Martha Berry Museum and Oak Hill, an 1847 plantation home with formal gardens, museum, and art gallery. A modest fee is charged to visit the museum. Martha Berry was a woman born to privilege who devoted her life to educating needy children, first in a tiny playhouse on the Oak Hill grounds, and then, with the help of philanthropists including Henry Ford and the labor of the students themselves, on the campus you see today.

Leave Berry College and travel north on US 27/GA 1 for 16 miles to Subligna Road. Turn right at a small shop. This road passes through open pasture and hay fields for about 8 miles to the small community of Subligna. This unusual name came about because an early settler named Underwood wanted to give the town his family name. Objection from other residents prompted him to suggest "Subligna," which was adopted. He coined the word from the two Latin root words *sub-* meaning "under" and *-lignum* meaning "wood." Mr. Underwood had the last laugh. There are two churches here, Baptist and Methodist. The Methodist church was established in 1855, just prior to the Civil War.

From Subligna, take the right fork in the road that leads for 10 miles to the community of Villanow. Taylor Ridge is on the left and Johns Mountain is on the right. At the junction of GA 136 is the Villanow General Store. This very old store is well worth a stop and short visit.

Turn right on GA 136 east and go through the low gap in Johns Mountain for about 0.5 mile to Pocket Rd. Turn right on Pocket Rd. You are now on the east side of Johns Mountain. In a short distance, about 3 miles, traveling past small residences, you enter the Armuchee District of Chattahoochee

Drive 3: Rome and Berry College to Villanow Loop

Johns Mountain and The Pocket

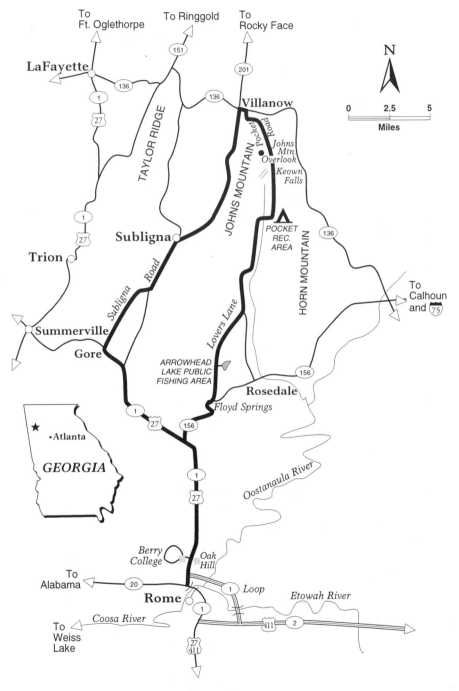

To Ft. Oglethorpe

To Ringgold

To Rocky Face

N

151

LaFayette

136

201

136

Villanow

0   2.5   5

Miles

1

27

TAYLOR RIDGE

Pocket Road

Johns Mtn. Overlook

Keown Falls

JOHNS MOUNTAIN

1

27

Subligna

POCKET REC. AREA

HORN MOUNTAIN

136

Trion

To Calhoun and 75

Subligna Road

Summerville

Lovers Lane

Gore

ARROWHEAD LAKE PUBLIC FISHING AREA

Rosedale

156

1

27

156

Floyd Springs

Atlanta

GEORGIA

1

27

Oostanaula River

Berry College

Oak Hill

To Alabama

20

1

Loop

Etowah River

Rome

1

Coosa River

411

2

To Weiss Lake

27
411

National Forest and the Johns Mountain Wildlife Management Area. Forest Road 208, about 0.5 mile on the right after you pass the Chattahoochee National Forest sign, leads to Johns Mountain Overlook. This gravel road, about 1.5 miles long, ends at the parking area for the overlook. From the large wooden platform you have a grand view of the ridges and valleys to the west. Taylor Ridge is the first, and depending on the visibility, you can see Pigeon and Lookout mountains of the Cumberland Plateau. This platform is on the Johns Mountain Trail that passes by Keown Falls.

Return to Pocket Rd., turn right, and in about a mile you come to the gravel Forest Road 702. It leads in less than a mile to Keown Falls Recreation Area, open from May 1 to October 31. Here you will find a parking area, picnic tables, comfort station, and the beginning of the 1.8-mile loop trail to Keown Falls. Should the gate be closed, as it is during the winter months, you can park at the gate and walk the 0.7-mile road to the recreation area and the trailhead for Keown Falls Trail. Camping is not permitted at this recreation area.

Back on Pocket Rd., turn right again. You are still in the valley between Horn Mountain and Johns Mountain. In 2 miles you come to the entrance of The Pocket Recreation Area. This campground is on the site of a former Civilian Conservation Corps camp with a spring that flows an estimated 12,000 gallons per hour. Campsites are equipped for RVs and tent camping. A fine picnic area and 2.6-mile hiking trail add much to this campground. The trail is noted for its abundance of spring wildflowers, especially a large colony of pink lady's-slipper orchids, which bloom in mid-April. The area is surrounded on three sides by mountains, hence the name "The Pocket."

Very near The Pocket is Lake Marvin. This is a pay-fishing lake with fine populations of bluegill and bass. Rental boats and other accessories are available. Lake Martin is also the site of the North Georgia Girl Scout Camp. The turnoff to this lake is about 0.5 mile from The Pocket.

Pocket Rd. continues down the narrow valley of Johns Creek, a seasonal trout stream. The winding road parallels Johns Creek and crosses it twice. At about 2.5 miles, you go in and out of the Johns Mountain Wildlife Management Area; in another 2.5 miles, you come to the junction of Everett Springs Road and Lovers Lane. Turn right on Lovers Lane at the Touchstone Brothers Store. Follow this road for 5.1 miles to the Arrowhead Public Fishing Area and the office for the Game Management Section of Georgia Wildlife Resources Division. At this area are two fishing lakes, ponds from the old fish hatchery, and the easy 2.2-mile Arrowhead Wildlife Interpretive Trail. A resident population of Canada geese nest here along with other water birds, including colorful wood ducks.

Old Mill Wheel, Berry College.

Ford Buildings, Berry College.

Continue on the paved road for 2.2 miles to Floyd Springs Road and another mile to GA 156. At this point, you can close the loop by turning right and going to US 27, about 2 miles, then left or south for about 7.5 miles on US 27 back to Rome.

If you prefer not to close the loop, you can add a pleasant drive through the Ostanaula River valley by turning left (not right) on GA 156, which leads to Calhoun in about 16 miles. I-75 is then about 1 mile from Calhoun.

4

Cedartown to Summerville

General description: This drive follows Georgia Highway 100 for about 50 miles passing across the wide valley of the Coosa River. It begins at Cedartown, passes through Cave Spring, and ends at Summerville.

Special attractions: Small-town Georgia, Cave Spring with a number of national historic buildings, James H. Floyd State Park, and peaceful rural scenery.

Location: Western edge of Georgia in the northwest corner.

Drive route numbers: GA 100 is the main route, except for a side visit to Cave Spring.

Travel season: Spring and fall are the most colorful seasons. Snow is infrequent and summer temperatures are moderate. This drive has attractions all year.

Camping: Camping facilities at James H. Floyd State Park, near Summerville.

Services: Lodging and food are available in Cedartown, Cave Spring, and Summerville. Hearn Academy Inn in Cave Spring is a 150-year-old bed and breakfast inn operated by the historical society.

Nearby attractions: Arrowhead Public Fishing Area; Floyd Springs; Summerville State Fish Hatchery; Weiss Lake in Alabama; and many attractions in nearby Rome.

 The drive

From Cedartown to Summerville, GA 100 meanders along the western side of the state, swinging past fields and forests, over rolling hills, and through green valleys. This is a drive through small-town Georgia. Cedartown, the largest municipality on the highway, has a population of slightly more than 10,000. Cave Spring and Summerville are less than half that size.

Around Cedartown, the land is part of the Piedmont, changing to the Ridge and Valley region around the Coosa River. It is the southernmost section of the Ridge and Valley province, which extends north into Pennsylvania. As the land goes, so go the roads: most of the main routes here run from northeast to southwest, following valleys along waterways such as Big Cedar Creek and the Chattooga River.

Before whites settled this land, a succession of native peoples lived here, and the Creeks and Cherokees fought over it. During the War of 1812,

Drive 4: Cedartown to Summerville

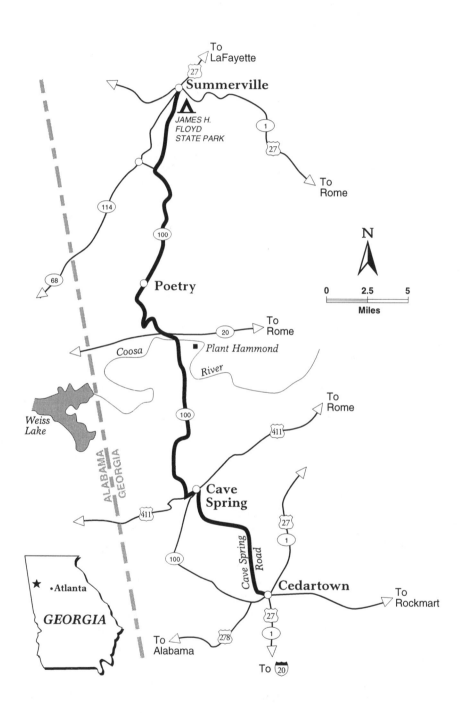

the Cherokees helped General Andrew Jackson fight the Creeks who had sided with the British. This area finally became part of the state of Georgia in 1838, when whites, coveting the fertile soil and mineral riches, forcibly removed the Indians.

This immediate area saw no major military action during the Civil War, though the battle of Chickamauga was fought only 30 miles north of Summerville and much of the campaign for Atlanta followed the Western and Atlantic Railroad tracks just 20 miles to the east. Drives 1, 2, and 3 are near this drive.

You can reach this route from Interstate 75 by following Georgia Highway 140 from Adairsville, joining U.S. Highway 27 North at Armuchee, and thence to Summerville. To reach Summerville from Interstate 65 in Alabama, follow Alabama Highway 117 east, where the road becomes Georgia Highway 48, and on to Summerville. From Interstate 20, you can reach Cedartown via either U.S. Highway 278 or 27, and follow their business routes into the city.

The drive begins in downtown Cedartown at the intersection of US 278 Bus. and 27 Bus. A self-guided tour map of Cedartown and Polk County is available from the Polk County Chamber of Commerce. Part of our drive is on that map. Go west on US 278 one block toward the brick First Methodist church. Jog right, then left between the Methodist church and the First Baptist Church. This puts you on Wissahickon Avenue. Behind the Methodist church is Big Spring, now housed in a Cedartown Water Department building (visitors welcome). This limestone spring, with an average flow of 12 million gallons per day, is the source of Cedartown's drinking water. It once was a ceremonial and gaming center for the Cherokees. Behind the waterworks building, Big Spring Park features a stream emanating from the spring. Across from the park, Cave Spring Street turns to the right. This is the old route of GA 100. It is an old-fashioned, narrow, curving road that undulates through Cedar Valley in Polk and Floyd counties. The new GA 100 runs to the west of it and is straighter and wider, but old GA 100 is the choice for charm.

At the edge of town is a grove of very old, large oak and pine trees, and on the right, the Peek Homeplace. It is a well-preserved plantation-style home built in 1866, complete with outbuildings. Farther on the left, a nineteenth-century brick home now hosts an antique store. Beyond that to the right is the John Pickett home, a two-story clapboard building with an impressive boxwood-lined drive. The age of this road is made evident by the vintage of the homes along it, as well as by its nature. In places, cedar trees line either side like hedgerows. The road follows the bottomland, paralleling small forest streams and skirting cattle pastures. The largest stream is Big Cedar Creek, which runs along the road starting about 2 miles out of Cedartown. This stream provided water power to run Sutton's

Mill at the intersection with Friendship Road. The remains of the mill, as well as a store and several homes, are indications that this at one time was a center of commerce for the farmers of the Friendship community.

As you cross the line into Floyd County, you will see an example of the logging practice known as clearcutting. Every tree in an area is cut down, and the stumps and roots are dug up by bulldozers. Sometimes the land is turned into pasture (or subdivisions), but often it is replanted in pine trees. Growing pines is considered a type of farming, like raising wheat or corn, but it takes twenty or more years for this crop to mature.

Ten miles from the start, you enter the community of Cave Spring, named for its water source, a free-flowing spring that issues from a cave near the center of town. The cave and spring are located in 29-acre Rolater Park, on your right as you enter town. This tree-shaded park has picnic tables, a large swimming pool, and a spring-fed trout pond. Feeding the trout is allowed, but fishing for them is not. There is a nominal charge to enter and explore the small cave. Its year-round 56-degrees-Fahrenheit coolness is especially welcome on hot summer days.

Cave Spring has more than ninety structures on the National Register of Historic Places, and its charming downtown has several antique stores, gift shops, and cafes. The town is also home of the Georgia School for the Deaf, founded in 1846 and still operating today. The school's buildings were used as a hospital during the Civil War.

At the traffic light in downtown Cave Spring, turn left onto Georgia Highway 53 and U.S. Highway 411. As you continue west, you will pick up GA 100. One mile later, turn right to follow GA 100 north.

A few miles up the road, you will cross Big Cedar Creek again, near Foster's Mill Store. Nine miles from Cave Spring, where the road tops a rise, a large smokestack juts up incongruously from the pastoral scenery. It is at Plant Hammond, a coal-fired steam generating plant owned by the Georgia Power Company. Adding to the irony of the scene is an ancient log cabin on the right. You can see the power plant itself as you cross the Coosa River.

Just past the river, turn left and pick up Georgia Highway 20. Continue for 3 miles and turn right, following GA 100. In this area, you will probably see kudzu. This fast-growing vine was introduced from Japan at the 1876 Centennial World's Fair. During the 1930s it was promoted as an effective way to control soil erosion. Its rapid growth quickly turned it into a nuisance, because it will cover fields, trees, and even houses in its path, if left unchecked.

Kinkaid Mountain rises to your left, and on the right is Simms Mountain. These are typical of the long ridges in this section of the country. Geologists say they were eroded from high mountains formed by the collision of the North American continent with Africa and Eurasia millions of years ago. The streams running through the valley flow into Weiss

Lake in Alabama. North of Holland is High Point, the southern end of Taylor Ridge. This highland, named for Cherokee Chief Richard Taylor, extends nearly 40 miles north to Ringgold, near the Tennessee border. Past High Point, Lyerly Dam Road leads left across the valley to the old mill town of Lyerly, now home to one of northwest Georgia's many carpet factories. The road leads to the ruins of a dam that once furnished water power to earlier mills here. Today the dam site is a popular fishing spot on the Chattooga River. Three miles north of Lyerly Dam Road, GA 100 crosses the Chattooga. This mention of the Chattooga River could cause some confusion with Georgia's other, more famous Chattooga River in the northeast corner of the state. The other one forms Georgia's northeast border with South Carolina, and its famous whitewater rapids were depicted in the film, *Deliverance*. The Chattooga River you are now crossing flows placidly to the southwest into Lake Weiss and Alabama's Coosa River. The two Chattoogas have no connection other than being in the same state.

A mile past the river, you enter the city limits of Summerville. Two miles later, GA 100 joins Georgia Highway 114 and continues to downtown Summerville. Both GA 100 and 114 end at their intersection with US 27.

Summerville, nestled in Broomtown Valley between Lookout Mountain and Taylor ridge, is noted for its many buildings decorated with murals celebrating the town's history and people. Pennville, just north of Summerville on US 27, is the home of noted visionary folk artist Howard Finster. His "Paradise Gardens" is built of wood, concrete, used bicycles, old tools, glass shards, and other items.

South of Summerville off US 27, James H. Floyd State Park offers picnicking, fishing, and camping. The many bluebird houses at the park and the numbers of bluebirds they have attracted have inspired similar birdhouse projects throughout the state. Menlo, 5 miles west of Summerville on GA 48, is home of a state fish hatchery, and is gateway to the scenic beauties of Lookout Mountain.

5

Land of the Cherokees

Calhoun and Etowah Mounds to New Echota

General description: From the edge of the Piedmont to the Ridge and Valley sections of the state, this 61-mile drive leads through the floodplain of the Etowah River, by the Etowah Mounds, through battlegrounds of the Civil War, and to the last town of the most advanced Native American culture, where the Cherokee language was taught and printed as the Cherokee newspaper, *The Cherokee Phoenix.* The towns are Cartersville, Stilesboro, Euharlee, Kingston, Adairsville, Calhoun, and, finally, New Echota, the historic capital of the Cherokee Nation.

Special attractions: Etowah Indian Mounds; Georgia Power Company's Bowen Steam Plant; Barnsley Gardens; historic Cartersville, Calhoun, and older small towns; the Western & Atlantic Railroad; New Echota; a covered bridge in Euharlee; Civil War history; beautiful fall colors; wildflowers; and carefully kept gardens.

Location: Northwest Georgia.

Drive route numbers: Interstate 75, Georgia Highway 113/61, Etowah Road, Old Mill Road, Covered Bridge Road, Shaw Street, Howard Street, Hall Station Road, Barnsley Gardens Road, Georgia Highway 140, U.S. Highway 41, and Georgia Highway 225.

Travel season: An all-season drive; most of the historic sites and gardens are open all year, except for Mondays, Christmas, and New Year's Day. Spring and fall are best for flowering trees, wildflowers, and fall leaf color.

Camping: Very limited camping on the drive proper. Red Top Mountain State Park and The Pocket Recreation Area on Chattahoochee National Forest, only a few miles from Calhoun, have fine campgrounds.

Services: Food and lodging are available in Cartersville and Calhoun and at several of the exits along I-75, which is paralleled on the drive.

Nearby attractions: Air Acres Museum in Cartersville, Allatoona Dam and Reservoir, William Weinman Mineral Museum, Confederate Cemetery and Battle of Resaca, Fort Mountain State Park, Chieftains Trail, Vann House Historic Site.

 The drive

This drive from Cartersville's Etowah Indian Mounds to New Echota near Calhoun covers a range of history, from Georgia's earliest inhabitants

Drive 5: Land of the Cherokees
Calhoun and Etowah Mounds to New Echota

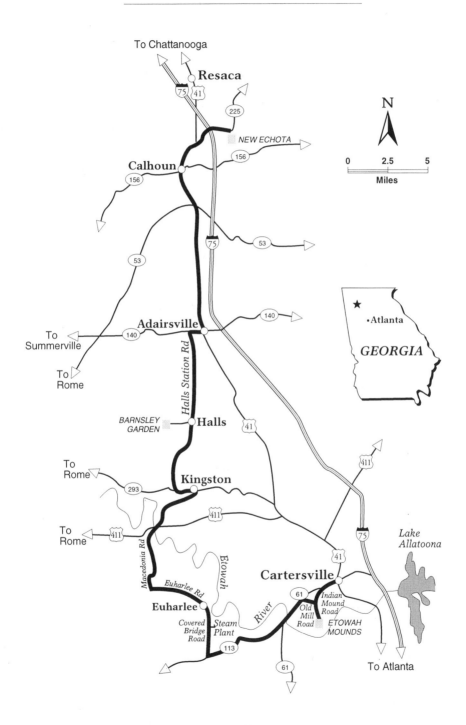

to Civil War sites to twentieth-century electricity production.

Cartersville, the starting point, has rich barite and ochre deposits. Barite, the ore of barium, is used in a number of products; ocher is a yellow mineral used mostly as a pigment. The William Weinman Mineral Museum has displays of local geology, as well as minerals from around the world, fossils, and Native American artifacts.

Much of the route is on secondary and tertiary roads linking villages such as Euharlee, Kingston, and Adairsville, along rolling countryside, skirting the tip of the Blue Ridge Mountains. You can reach either end of the route directly from I-75. Other drives nearby are Drive 2, 3, 7, and 8.

The drive begins at the GA 113 exit off I-75 (Exit 124), going west on GA 113 toward Cartersville. Continue on Georgia 113 (Main Street) straight across US 41.

Cartersville was built around the railroad tracks, which pass north and south through town; the old downtown business district is on a rectangular open area on either side of the tracks, with a brick depot building in the center. A self-guided walking tour is available at the Tourism Council on Main St.

Continue to follow GA 113 to where it turns right, and Etowah Drive goes straight. Pick up Etowah Dr. You should see signs directing you toward Etowah Mounds. Continue for 2.5 miles to the entrance to the mounds historic area. This pre-Columbian site by the Etowah River was a major city of Mississipian mound builders. It was occupied between A.D. 900 and 1500, by people who built several ceremonial earth mounds. The largest mound covers 3 acres and is 63 feet high. This state historic site also features a museum. You can climb stairways to the tops of the mounds and look over the floodplain which was farmed by the Indians hundreds of years ago. After marveling at the achievements of this civilization, head back toward Cartersville on Etowah Dr. To the left is Dellinger Park, a well-landscaped city park with trails and recreational facilities.

Turn left on Old Mill Road about 1.5 miles from the mounds, then turn left onto GA 61/113 and cross the Etowah River. The floodplain here is broad and flat, with cultivated fields and some industrial activity. To the right, you will soon see cooling towers of the Georgia Power Company's Plant Bowen. It is the sort of structure associated with nuclear power plants, but this steam generating facility is coal-fired.

When you get to Stilesboro, the structure on the hill to the left is Stilesboro Academy, a schoolhouse built in 1859. Half a mile past the academy, turn right on Covered Bridge Road. You are headed straight toward Plant Bowen. As you pass closely by the cooling tower, you realize how enormous it really is.

Two miles later, you are back a hundred years at Euharlee. This village, whose name is Cherokee for "she laughs as she runs," boasts the oldest remaining covered bridge in Georgia. Lowery (or Euharlee Creek) bridge was built in 1886 by Horace King, a noted black bridge builder. Numbers on the beams of the bridge indicate it was prefabricated elsewhere, brought here, and put together over the creek. The bridge is no longer open for vehicular traffic. It is located to the left of the current road. Go through the village and turn left on Euharlee Road. About 4 miles later, turn right on Macedonia Road at Old (1847) Macedonia Baptist Church. Two and a half miles later, turn right on U.S. Highway 411. You will almost immediately cross the Etowah River bridge and turn left off this four-lane highway toward Kingston on Reynolds Bridge Road. Follow Reynolds Bridge Rd. 2 miles into Kingston, and continue to Church Street, where you turn left, crossing the railroad tracks.

This sleepy railroad town was astir with action during the Civil War. In 1862, Federal raiders under James Andrews stole the Confederate locomotive *General* south of here at Kennesaw and passed through Kingston, intending to destroy rails and bridges behind them. Their plan was foiled by train conductor W. A. Fuller, who pursued the *General* 87 miles by foot, handcar, switch engine, and finally, the locomotive *Texas*. Andrews' Raiders were captured and hanged. Their actions made them the first recipients of the Congressional Medal of Honor. In 1864, federal troops under General William Tecumseh Sherman paused in Kingston three days before driving forward toward Atlanta. And on May 12, 1865, this was the spot of the last Confederate surrender east of the Mississippi. Lee's surrender at Appomatox

Etowah Mounds Historic Site, near Cartersville.

had taken place more than a month earlier. The Confederate Memorial Museum on Main Street is open by appointment.

At the intersection with Howard St. (GA 293), turn left, then turn right onto Halls Station Road. The railroad on the right is the state-owned Western & Atlantic Railroad (now operated by CSX). It is the reason for Atlanta being where it is, because Atlanta was the southern terminus to this road, which was the first rail link between the Mississippi River Valley with the Atlantic Seaboard. It was also the railroad along which General Sherman's Atlanta Campaign was fought during the Civil War. On the left, Connesena Creek parallels the road.

Five miles up Halls Station Rd., Barnsley Gardens Road on the left leads to Barnsley Gardens, 2.5 miles away. A wealthy Savannah merchant, Godfrey Barnsley, built a home here in the 1840s. The ruins of his mansion have been preserved, and his extensive gardens have been restored. Five miles north on Halls Station Rd. is Adairsville. The depot here is where Captain Fuller boarded the locomotive *Texas* during The Great Locomotive Chase of Andrews' Raiders. Turn right on GA 140 east, then left on US 41. This four-lane highway was once a main north-south artery, but is now replaced by I-75, which parallels it to the east. US 41 still carries a fair amount of traffic, most of it local people and shunpikers. Continue 10 miles on US 41 to Calhoun, then through the town to GA 225, where you turn right, pass under I-75, and a mile later arrive at the entrance to New Echota His-

Ruins of the Godfrey Barnsley Mansion at Barnsley Gardens.

Lowery (or Euharlee Creek) Bridge in Euharlee.

toric Site. From 1825 to 1838, this was the capitol of the Cherokee Nation. The Cherokee Supreme Court building still stands, as does a missionary's house and the shop that published *The Cherokee Phoenix*, a newspaper printed in the Cherokee alphabet invented by Sequoyah. This historic site is also where the New Echota Treaty of 1835 was signed that resulted, three years later, in the infamous "Trail of Tears" on which the Cherokee people were forcibly rounded up and marched to Oklahoma.

Drive 6: Cohutta Wilderness Loop

Chatsworth to Lake Conasauga to Fort Mountain

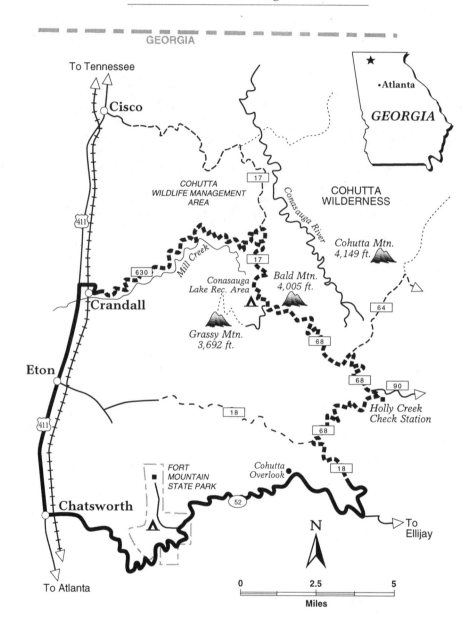

6

Cohutta Wilderness Loop
Chatsworth to Lake Conasauga to Fort Mountain

General description: A 75-mile drive that takes you from Chatsworth along the edge of the Cohutta Wilderness Area, by the Conasauga Lake Recreation Area and campground in the Chattahoochee National Forest, and to Fort Mountain State Park. Most of the drive is in national forest. Hiking, birding, fishing, hunting, and viewing beautiful wildflowers and mountains make this an adventure as well as a scenic drive. About half of the drive is on winding, gravel Forest Service roads. Some of the way is steep; if you are traveling in an RV or pulling a camping trailer it is advisable to check with the Forest Service's Cohutta Ranger District office in Chatsworth before you drive up the mountain (address and phone number in the appendix).

Special attractions: Mountain scenery all along the way, especially at several strategically located overlooks; flowering trees and shrubs; fall leaf color; a wide variety of hiking trails; fine campsites; trout fishing; and hunting in season.

Location: North Georgia near the Tennessee state line.

Drive route numbers: U.S. Highway 411; Grassy Road; Mill Creek Road; Forest Roads 630, 17, 68, and 18; and Georgia Highway 52.

Travel season: All year, except for occasional snows that make it necessary for the Forest Service to close roads for short periods of time. April through June is best for most flowering shrubs, trees, and wildflowers. Fall leaf color begins at the higher elevations in late September. During the winter when the leaves are off the trees, the mountain views are more exposed.

Camping: More than 30 campsites are open from mid-April to mid-October at Lake Conasauga Recreation Area. Fort Mountain State Park has more than 70 tent and trailer sites and 15 cottages. Primitive camping is permitted in Chattahoochee National Forest.

Services: Motels, restaurants, and gas are available in and near Chatsworth. Cohutta Lodge, offering rooms, meals, gift shops, and other amenities, is located on GA 52 near the entrance to Fort Mountain State Park.

Nearby attractions: Vann House west of Chatsworth; whitewater rafting at the Ocoee River, which is the 1996 Olympic kayaking venue just across the state line in Tennessee; Carters Lake; and the Cohutta Wilderness Area, largest mountain wilderness in the East, at 35,000 acres.

 # The drive

This loop drive begins at Chatsworth, climbs along Mill Creek, skirts the edge of the Cohutta Wilderness, swings around for a look at Fort Mountain's mysterious rock walls, and returns to Chatsworth. It is short in mileage, but since most of the drive is on dirt and gravel roads, you should be traveling slowly. Give yourself plenty of time.

Before you start, check with the USDA Forest Service office in Chatsworth for advice and the latest conditions. *Nota Bene* to drivers of cars with low ground clearance, RVs, and pullers of travel trailers: A large part of this drive is on Forest Service roads. They are dirt or gravel, are narrow, winding, steep in places, and may be in poor condition depending on the weather and maintenance schedules.

The Cohutta Mountains, part of the Blue Ridge mountain chain, loom 2,800 feet above the Great Valley. Most of the land is part of the Chattahoochee National Forest. The Cohutta Wilderness is the largest of sixteen areas given wilderness status by the Wilderness Act of 1975. Its 35,000 acres lie in northern Georgia and southern Tennessee. Hikers will enjoy the challenge of walking the rugged terrain, and anglers will find rainbow, brown, and brook trout in the Conasauga and Jacks rivers and their tributaries.

This drive is near four other drives: Drives 2, 5, 7, and 8. Interstate highway access is via U.S. Highway 76 or GA 52 from Dalton.

The drive begins at the intersection of GA 52 with US 411 in downtown Chatsworth. Head north on US 411. You are driving through the Great

Cohutta Wilderness Area from Grassy Mountain fire tower.

Valley between the Cohutta Mountains and the Armuchee Ridges. It has been a corridor of travel since the earliest American Indians came here thousands of years ago. Beginning in 1805, it was the eastern fork of the Federal Road, a postal route through the Cherokee Nation to Knoxville, Tennessee. To the right are the Cohutta Mountains. You can see a fire lookout tower, tiny in the distance on the peak of Grassy Mountain (elevation 3,692). It sits above the Conasauga Lake Recreation Area run by the Forest Service.

Pass through the small town of Eton, (pronounced EE-tahn) about 3 miles farther. At Crandall, about 7 miles into the drive, look on the right for Grassy Rd.. Turn right on Grassy Rd. go about a quarter mile and cross the CSX railroad tracks. After you cross the tracks, turn right, go a block, then turn left on Mill Creek Road (Forest Road 630). You are going up the mountains along Mill Creek. Part of the road surface will be bare rock, practically guaranteed to be rough and bumpy. Think of it as an opportunity to drive slowly enough to enjoy the forest. It is a real treat in the summertime to drive with the car windows down, because mountain temperatures are usually several degrees cooler than the flatlands below. During spring, the wildflowers will be numerous, and in fall, the leaf color can be spectacular.

At the top of the ridge, some 10 miles up FR 630, turn right at the intersection and up the steep slope onto Forest Road 17. Straight ahead is parking for the Hickory Creek trailhead into the Cohutta Wilderness. The wilderness is closed to vehicles in order to preserve its wild, rugged, and natural character. From 1915 to 1935, 70 percent of this area was logged. What you are seeing is second-growth forest. Naturalists have identified more than forty rare and uncommon plants in this wilderness, which is also home to white-tailed deer, black bear, and wild hogs.

A mile up FR 17 is Mill Creek Overlook, a wide (comparatively) spot in the road where you can stop and admire the westward view over the Great Valley towards Dalton and Rocky Face Ridge. From here it is 1.5 miles to the junction with Forest Road 68. To the right, 0.5 mile away, is Conasauga Lake Recreation Area and Campground.

Operated by the Forest Service, it is a popular spot, particularly when the weather is hot elsewhere. Conasauga Lake was built in the 1930s by the Civilian Conservation Corps. At over 3,100 feet above sea level, it is the highest lake in the state, and offers swimming as well as fishing for trout, bluegill, and bass.

To the left from the junction with FR 17, FR 68 continues around the rim of the wilderness area, through a gap between Bald Mountain (on the left) and Little Bald Mountain (on the right), and then onto Cohutta Mountain.

Pass a couple of parking areas for trails going into the wilderness area. Tearbritches Creek Trail is about 0.5 mile past the FR 17 junction, and Chestnut Lead Trail is about 1.5 miles past that. (A "lead" is a local term for a

A section of stone wall of unknown origin in Fort Mountain State Park.

mountain spur.)

Four miles from the FR 17 junction, turn right. You are continuing to follow FR 68 at its junction with Forest Road 64. FR 64 is the road in front of you. FR 68 descends Potatopatch Mountain. You may want to shift to a lower gear—this is a long downslope. The Forest Service usually recommends that recreational vehicles and travel trailers go up and down FR 630 when visiting Conasauga Lake.

Three miles from the junction is an unimproved overlook, a break in the trees partially caused by tornado damage and partly by logging. Just beyond is an improved overlook with a parking turnout and a beautiful view south. On a clear day, it is said you can see Atlanta.

Barnes Creek Picnic Area, 0.5 mile farther, is a good place to stop for a closeup look at wildflowers blooming here. Early spring brings trilliums, jack-in-the-pulpits, and foam flowers; in summer, the roadsides are decorated with fire pinks, oswego tea, brown-eyed Susan, and many others. Continue on FR 68, bearing right at the junction with Forest Road 90, through Holly Creek Gap, and past the Holly Creek Check Station, which is a control point for the Cohutta Wildlife Management Area, a state-managed hunting area. Hunters check in and out here, giving Department of Natural Resources rangers control over the number of hunters in the area and giving wild game biologists an idea of the number of animals taken. In less than 0.5 mile, you begin to see cabins built on private land along Holly Creek.

Two miles past the check station, turn left on Forest Road 18. Following FR 18 to the right will take you through the valley of Holly Creek to US

411 at Eton. We want to go left, through Mulberry Gap. You will know you are on the right road if you pass an old fire truck on the right about 1.5 miles later.

Nearly a mile past the fire truck, you return to paved road surface, and a mile later, turn right on GA 52. In 3 miles, a turnout to the right leads to Cohutta Overlook. This is a small park with paved parking and a stone-walled overlook. It is an excellent site for a picnic, especially with the view of the mountains to the north. The Grassy Mountain fire tower, in the distance, gives you an idea of how far you have come. Three miles down GA 52 is a less elaborate overlook, and 1 mile past that is the entrance to Fort Mountain State Park. It is 2 miles to parking for the old stone "fort." An 855-foot-long piled rock wall here has been known since earliest times. No one knows what it really is, who built it, or why, but there are a number of theories. Some say it was built by Hernando de Soto's expedition in the 1600s. Some say it was built as a worship site by American Indians, and some say it was an Indian honeymoon haven. You are free to accept or reject any of these theories, or make up your explanation. In addition to the mystery of the fort, the park offers camping, hiking, and water sports at the park lake.

A half mile past the park entrance is another overlook were the road leads down the mountain and out of Chattahoochee National Forest. You soon start to encounter homes and businesses as you near Chatsworth. This is the county seat of Murray County, and you can see the courthouse as you top a rise coming into town and return to the starting point, the intersection of GA 52 with US 411.

7

Georgia Foothills Loop
Canton to Ellijay to Amicalola Falls to Tate

General description: For 105 miles, this drive travels over paved rural roads through small towns and on four-lane divided highways with views of the ridges and mountains of north Georgia. You ride through foothills to the southern edge of the Blue Ridge Mountains at Amicalola Falls State Park. Marble deposits near Tate and Nelson are the world's largest and best quality.

Special attractions: Spring flowers and beautiful fall colors, without the heavy traffic of the eastern part of the mountains; apple orchards and apple houses where fruit can be bought in late summer and fall; marble production in Tate; the Tate House, a pink marble mansion with restaurant, bed and breakfast, and cabins; Amicalola Falls State Park with the highest falls east of the Mississippi River; and the start of the southern approach trail to the Appalachian Trail.

Location: North Georgia.

Drive route numbers: Interstate 575, Georgia Highways 5, 140, 372, 515 (Zell Miller Mountain Parkway), 52, 138, 136, and 53.

Travel season: Fall is most colorful, with apple-picking from August through October. Marble quarries and Georgia Marble Works are open only during the Marble Festival in October, for specific dates, call ahead (see the appendix).

Camping: Amicalola Falls State Park with tent, RV camping, and cabins; several U.S. Army Corps of Engineers recreation areas at Carters Lake (see Drive 8).

Services: Good restaurants in Tate, Jasper, and Ellijay; Amicalola Falls State Park and Lodge with rooms and buffet-style dining room overlooking grand mountain views; lodging, bed and breakfasts, and private campgrounds are along the route.

Nearby attractions: Dahlonega Gold Museum; Bill Elliott racing garages near Dawsonville; John's Mill near Hinton; Carters Lake; Fort Mountain State Park; North Georgia Mountains; Lake Lanier; Allatoona Lake; and Red Top Mountain State Park.

Drive 7: Georgia Foothills Loop
Canton to Ellijay to Amicalola Falls to Tate

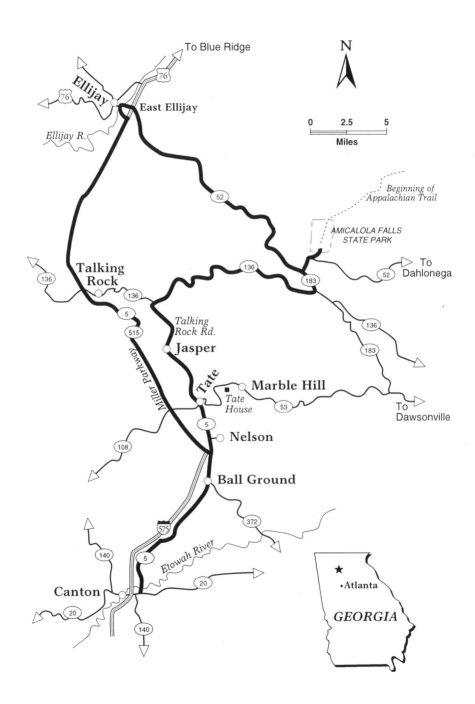

To Blue Ridge

N

Ellijay

East Ellijay

Ellijay R.

0   2.5   5
Miles

Beginning of
Appalachian Trail

AMICALOLA FALLS
STATE PARK

Talking
Rock

To
Dahlonega

Talking
Rock Rd.

Jasper

Tate

Marble Hill

Tate
House

To
Dawsonville

Miller Parkway

Nelson

Ball Ground

Etowah River

Canton

Atlanta

GEORGIA

# The drive

This is a drive that offers several alternate drive opportunities. The route chosen takes you on the mountain parkway, through apple country, and into several small north Georgia towns, each with its own unique atmosphere.

The suggested beginning is on the north side of Canton, where I-575 Exit 11 takes you to old GA 5. This is the first right turn off the exit ramp and begins a two-lane paved road. From here it is about 6.5 miles to the city limits of Ball Ground. Don't expect to see a town here because you are traveling through an area of small farms and wooded hillsides. In about one mile you pick up GA 372, which comes in from the right.

The old town of Ball Ground is off the highway to the east. The name comes from the location of a Cherokee Indian ground used to play a game similar to lacrosse. Indians referred to the game as "the brother of war" because it was played with great ferocity and was a substitute for actual battles between tribes. This is also the site of the great Battle of Taliwa between the Creek and Cherokee Indians about 1755. Cherokees drove the Creeks south of the Chattahoochee River, which became the boundary line between the two nations until the "Trail of Tears" era, when the Cherokees v here driven to Oklahoma.

Very shortly you come to a left turn that is marked GA 372 and GA 5 Bus. This road merges into the four-lane that becomes the Zell Miller Mountain Parkway. Unlike the older roads that followed the valleys of least resistance, this new highway travels along and over ridges, giving you a much better view of the surroundings. In about 1.5 miles you merge with what appears to be another expressway but is actually the end of I-575 and the continuation of the Mountain Parkway, which is also designated GA 5 and 515. If you had stayed on I-575 at Canton, you would come to this same place. We drove the old highway to Ball Ground in order to give a better taste of the rural countryside in north Georgia.

The parkway bypasses the small towns. There are a few traffic lights where smaller state highways cross. The first one is at the intersection with Georgia Highway 108, which goes to Tate. In another 5.5 miles you cross GA 53. Three miles further you will see, first on the right and then on both sides, an area without large trees. This resulted from a forestry practice called clearcutting. The hardwood trees are completely removed, and pines trees are planted for pulpwood. It takes about twenty years to grow the first crop.

Cuts through the ridges are sloping banks that have healed over with a thick cover of vegetation. In spring, many kinds of wildflowers bloom on these banks. Early summer will bring the oxeye daisies in profusion. During the summer, many of the banks will be covered with kudzu, a vine that

This marker at the visitor center in Amicalola Falls State Park is the common southern beginning for many who hike the Appalachian Trail.

engulfs everything in its path. Where it has become well established, trees will be completely covered and will eventually die. On the ground, it is a very effective erosion-control plant, but it can get out of hand. In spring and early summer, the highway median is a sea of blossoming poppies, bachelor buttons, and crimson clover, thanks to a beautification project by the Georgia Department of Transportation.

Dogwood and redbud trees begin blooming in April. Azaleas, under the hardwood trees, bloom in late April and May. In early spring, the great variety of deciduous trees begin to leaf out, and the different shades of green for each species make the forest almost as pretty as in fall. In July, the sourwood trees show the white clusters of flowers used by honey bees to produce sourwood mountain honey. Fall leaf color begins in mid-October and some years lasts for two or three weeks.

The only interruption to the mixed hardwood-pine forest on the ridgesides is the small businesses that have become established at the intersections.

About 2 miles past where GA 136 turns off the parkway is the only scenic overlook in this section of the road. In about 10 miles, after passing the Gilmer County line and Georgia Highway 382, you come to an intersection with traffic light, several fast-food restaurants, and other businesses. This is where U.S. Highway 76 enters from the west. Continue to the next

Tate House mansion and restaurant built entirely
of pink marble. A bed and breakfast inn today.

traffic light and turn to the left, cross the Ellijay River, and immediately turn to the right on GA 52, a two-lane paved highway. You are now going upstream along the Ellijay River, which is right beside the road. In about 1 mile you go under the parkway overpass. An access road that turns off here goes to US 76.

Traveling east on GA 52, you come into the heart of apple country. Your first indications are roadside packing sheds, or apple houses, where you can buy the fruit. Orchards of small, bushy apple trees visible from the road are usually associated with the applehouses. However, most of the orchards are on the ridges out of sight of the road.

Apple season begins in August and continues into November. The apple houses usually have more than fruit, and are interesting places to stop to see some of the other local foods for sale, including honey, canned jams and jellies, pickled beans, fried apple pies, and locally made apple bread, as well as craft items and antique farm implements.

Beside apples and a few nectarines and peaches, cattle and poultry are the main farm products. Rolling pasture adds to the scenic beauty of this section. The higher ridges are covered with hardwood forests, and in the valleys are a few fields of corn and some cabbage.

Oakland Academy, on the right about 8 miles from Ellijay, was established in 1867 and became the educational center for the surrounding area. It has changed operation and ownership several times and is now operated by Gilmer County.

The few homes that can be seen along the road are well kept, with neat flowerbeds and nicely landscaped yards.

GA 52 is truly a foothills highway, going from Dalton eastward through Ellijay to Dahlonega and on east to GA 365 expressway beyond Gainesville. This is an especially good section to see spring flowers, flowering trees, and fall leaf color.

It is about 28 miles from Ellijay to the junction of GA 183. From late spring to early fall, you will see great patches of kudzu growing along the road banks and over many of the trees.

Stay on GA 52 for another 2 miles to the entrance to Amicalola Falls State Park. About half way there, you pass Burt's Farm. In the fall, this is one of the largest displays of pumpkins in the state.

As you drive into the park, you pass the visitor center on the right and continue straight ahead to the foot of the falls. This is the highest falls east of the Mississippi, a series of cascades with a total drop of 729 feet down the steep rocky face. There is parking and a turnaround here. Coming back to the visitor center, take the road to the right to go to the top of the mountain and to the lodge, restaurant, and campground. This steep, 0.5-mile drive is prohibited to trailers more than 16 feet long. The parking area at the top of the falls is on the right. Go straight ahead to get to the lodge or turn to the left to go to the campground and cabins.

There are several hiking trails in the park, but the the 8-mile-long approach trail to Springer Mountain is the best known, for it is the southern terminus of the Appalachian Trail. At the visitor center, long-term parking is available to those planning to hike the Appalachian Trail. The lodge is a well-equipped hotel and buffet-style restaurant with a grand view of the surrounding mountains and valleys.

To continue the drive, go back down the steep hill. You are advised to use low gear on the way down. Back at GA 52, turn right and retrack to GA 183. A little more than a mile farther is the intersection with GA 136; turn right. In about 1.5 miles, pass Faucet Lake on the right. This is a small but quite attractive lake impounded by the road fill. GA 136 continues as a winding road up Burnt Mountain. In 4.5 miles, you reach the top and cross the Pickens County line. This is all private land with considerable residential development—mostly as retirement or second homes. From the county line, it is about 2.5 miles to an overlook on the left with space for about four or five vehicles. Another overlook is 1.5 miles farther. The road is now dropping down the mountain and into the narrow valley. About a mile farther, GA 136 makes a right angle turn to the right. At this point, you have the option of following GA 136 to Talking Rock and then to Jasper, or you can continue straight ahead on Burnt Mountain Road and come to Jasper in about 6.5 miles.

Going to Talking Rock on GA 136, there is a sharp left turn at about 2 miles. In another 2 miles, you come to an intersection with a small white church. Turn left, still following GA 136, and you come to the community of Talking Rock. The old buildings are reminiscent of the days when this was a regular railroad stop. Cross the railroad tracks and come to another intersection where you turn left on Talking Rock Road and go to Jasper. GA 136 turns to the right.

In 5 miles you come to the Jasper city limits and 0.5 mile farther you come to a black wooden bridge on the left that crosses the railroad track. Across this bridge is the Woodbridge Inn, a restaurant and lodge that is a favorite for people from all over north Georgia. If you chose to go straight to Jasper instead of going around by Talking Rock you do not pass Woodbridge Inn, but it is only a few blocks to the north when you reach downtown Jasper.

About 7 miles west of Jasper, toward Hinton, is John's Mill, an old restored water-powered grist mill that still makes stone-ground corn meal. There is the original stone dam, wooden flume, and log cabins. It is open on weekends.

From Jasper, this drive continues for 5 miles on GA 53 East to Tate. At Tate, you turn left (to the east), and stay on GA 53. This is the heart of

Georgia's marble industry. On GA 53, pass the Tate railroad station, cross the tracks, and continue on the winding road past the gray marble Tate Elementary School. A little farther on, you come to the Tate House, a mansion built of pink marble. This is a bed and breakfast inn, with restaurant and log cabin cottages. On the grounds behind the Tate House are the offices of the Georgia Marble Company, the world's largest producer of marble. For safety reasons, the enormous quarries and massive gang saws cannot ordinarily be open to the public; however, tours are conducted during the Marble Festival each October. Reservations are suggested (for the phone number, see the appendix).

Return to Tate and turn left (south), and continue 4 miles past Nelson, where there is more marble production, and another 4 miles to Ball Ground. This closes the loop. The turnoff to I-575 is about 2 miles farther. I-575 South returns to Canton.

As mentioned above, this drive lends itself to several side trips. If you continue on the Zell Miller Parkway past Ellijay, you can go to Blue Ridge and Blairsville on US 76, or to McCaysville and Copperhill, Tennessee, on GA 5. Just beyond Blue Ridge, GA 60 goes to Suches and Dahlonega (see Drive 9). From Dahlonega, you can travel GA 52 to Amicalola Falls State Park. Another possible trip continues eastward on GA 52 from Amicalola Falls State Park and on to Dahlonega. For still another option, you can continue east on GA 183 from GA 52 and go to Dawsonville, the home of the Bill Elliott Garages.

Drive 8: Carters Lake Loop
Ellijay to Ellijay

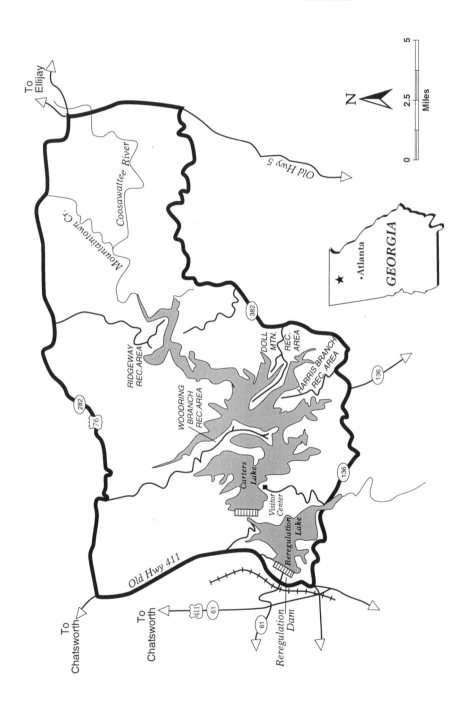

8

Carters Lake Loop
Ellijay to Ellijay

General description: Beginning at Ellijay, this drive encircles scenic Carters Lake and leads through the steep ridges and narrow valleys at the southern end of the higher Blue Ridge Mountains. You can visit the powerhouse and reregulating reservoir as well as the dam; the visitor center overlooks the lake and surrounding mountains. This convoluted terrain supports a wide variety of forest trees and flowering plants.

Special attractions: Although the reservoir is not visible for most of the drive, it can be seen from several points. Activities include camping, fishing in the two lakes and several streams nearby, hiking, boating, swimming, and a variety of other outdoor activities associated with the lake and adjacent Corps of Engineers property. Hunting is allowed in season on Coosawattee Wildlife Management Area. Also visit the Carters Dam Powerhouse, its unusual reversible pump-turbines, and its reregulating resevoir.

Location: North-central Georgia.

Drive route numbers: U.S. Highway 76, Old U.S. Highway 411, Georgia Highways 136 and 382, and Old Georgia Highway 5.

Travel season: Except during rare heavy winter snowfalls, this drive is open all year. Each season is interesting, unique, and adds variety to the drive.

Camping: The U.S. Army Corps of Engineers has campgrounds at the Woodring Branch, Doll Mountain, Harris Branch, and Ridgeway recreation areas. Woodring Branch and Doll Mountain have trailer and tent camping. Harris Branch and Ridgeway are equipped for tent camping only.

Services: Excellent restaurants, hotels, and motels in Ellijay and Chatsworth, as well as in the smaller towns like Blue Ridge, Cherry Log, and Jasper. Several picnic areas are located around the lake. The Carters Lake Marina and Resort is the only commercial facility on the lake shore. It provides lake shore cabins, boat rental, boat launching ramp, and boat slips.

Nearby attractions: Fort Mountain State Park; apple houses on most of the highways into Ellijay; Vann House Historic Site; Chattahoochee National Forest; Cohutta Wilderness Area; Benton MacKaye Trail; fishing in Carters Lake and in the river below the dam; trout fishing in several nearby cold mountain streams; and Ridgeway Mountain Bike Trail.

The drive

This drive makes a loop around Carters Lake, one of the most beautiful lakes in the Southeast. Ironically, the lake itself is never actually visible from the road, but gorgeous lake vistas amply reward travelers who visit Carters recreation areas and scenic overlooks. Completed in 1977 after fifteen years of construction, this U.S. Army Corps of Engineers project impounds the Coosawattee River. The deep, clear waters of Carters Lake offer boating, swimming, and fishing. Though only 11 miles long, the lake has a shoreline of more than 60 miles, with numerous inlets. Federal regulations prohibit private docks on the lake, or any alteration of the shoreline, and the government owns a minimum of 300 feet from the water's edge, ensuring that the sparkling waters will continue to reflect forest margins as a scenic delight for visitors. The lake is named not, as you might assume, for former President Jimmy Carter of Georgia, but for the community of Carters Quarters, located near the dam. Farrish Carter, for whom the community was named, was a wealthy landowner here in the middle nineteenth century.

Beginning and ending in Ellijay, and easily reached from Interstate 75 via Interstate 575 and GA 5 (Zell Miller Mountain Parkway), the route leads through a section of the Blue Ridge Mountains, past Brushy Top and Buck Knob mountains, to the rich lowlands once farmed by the Cherokee; and near Fort Gilmer, where these native people were confined before being marched to Oklahoma in the infamous Trail of Tears. Visiting the dam and powerhouse, the drive then swings back through the mountains, past recreation areas on the lake shore, to return to Ellijay.

Four other drives are nearby: Drives 2, 5, 6, and 7.

The drive begins in Ellijay at the intersection of GA 5 and Maddox Drive. GA 5, the four-lane Zell Miller Mountain Parkway, scoots you to the mountains from I-75 via I-575 north of Marietta. The intersection is marked by fast-food emporia and gas stations. Follow Maddox Dr. to the next traffic light, where you pick up U.S. Highway 76 West. Continue straight ahead. The road soon rises and begins to curve; this is the southernmost portion of the Blue Ridge Mountains, which run along the eastern edge of the Appalachian system to southeastern Pennsylvania. The road curves pleasantly through the mixed pine and hardwood forest, passing modest homes that range from neat cottages to what can charitably be called "mountain cabins" to mobile homes.

Ellijay and Gilmer County are the best-known areas of apple production in Georgia. Though the majority of orchards are east of Ellijay, there are a few apple-packing sheds along this route. In the late summer and through autumn, apple varieties such as Rome, Delicious, Arkansas Black, Yates,

Carters Lake and Dam from visitor center overlook

and Winesap are shipped throughout the country. Apple lovers flock to these "apple houses" to buy fruit fresh from the orchard.

Mountaintown Creek, which you cross about 5 miles into the drive, flows from Pine Knob on Betty Mountain in the Chattahoochee National Forest, and empties into Carters Lake. Many of the roads of North Georgia follow the hillsides beside creek bottoms. Early immigrants arriving here in the 1830s and 1840s chose this bottomland as the most desirable place to farm. It is relatively flat, and the soil is comparatively rich. These pioneers built their cabins at the foot of the mountains, and the roads typically ran above the fields, following the contours of the lower slopes. Most rural roads in the area still do.

Some 2 miles past Mountaintown Creek is the road leading left to Ridgeway Recreation Area and Coosawattee Wildlife Management Area. The Corps of Engineers operates a total of eight public areas around the lake. Some of the areas, particularly campgrounds, are closed during the winter months, so check before you plan your activities (see the appendix). Coosawattee WMA is operated by the Georgia Department of Natural Resources as a place for public hunting and outdoor recreation.

Continuing on US 76, cross Tails Creek below Brushy Top, pass the entrance to Woodring Branch Recreation Area, and about 15 miles from your starting point, round a bend on Buck Knob where the roadbed has been blasted through granite, and come upon your first view of the Great Valley beyond the mountains. In the distance you can see across the

Conasauga and Coosawattee rivers to Horn and Rocky Face mountains in the Armuchee Ridges, 20 miles away near Dalton. At the bottom of the slope, you will arrive at a T intersection. Turn left here, off US 76 and onto Old U.S. Highway 411. This highway is called Old US 411 but it is also the old Federal Road. The current US 411 was relocated west of here in the 1970s. This road was here long before highways were given numbers, and was the first vehicular route to join Tennessee and Georgia through the Cherokee Nation, following an older Indian trading path to Athens and Augusta. In 1803, the Cherokees granted the United States the right to use this path into the America beyond the mountains. Just north of this point at modern-day Ramhurst, the road forked. The east fork of the road went to Knoxville, Tennessee, and the west fork went to Nashville.

In less than a mile after your turn, you come to Fort Gilmer. The discovery of gold in North Georgia and pressure by whites to settle this area resulted in a number of treaties with the Creeks and Cherokees, ceding Indian land to the state. Finally, the New Echota Treaty of 1835 swapped the last Cherokee lands here for land in Oklahoma. A historic marker indicates the location of this fort, built in 1838 to enforce the removal of the Cherokee from this area. General Winfield Scott was in charge of herding the reluctant Indians together at Fort Gilmer and forcing them to march through winter storms to their new home in the West. This journey, during which thousands of Cherokees died, is called the Trail of Tears. The road here undulates through the valley bottom, through lush pastures and stands of large trees. On the right is the nineteenth-century home of Farrish Carter, for whom, indirectly, the lake is named. It is a private home, not open to the public. As you continue the drive, the large barns in this valley are evidence that this bottomland has been rich farming country for a long time.

About 4 miles from the turn onto Old US 411 is the road leading some 2 miles to Carters Dam Powerhouse. The U.S. Army Corps of Engineers keeps this road well tended and parklike, with wide, grassy shoulders. At 445 feet, Carters Dam is the highest in Georgia, forming the state's deepest lake. To your right as you approach the dam, you will see the reregulation impoundment, an assistant reservoir for Carters Lake. Water that turns generators in the powerhouse flows into this smaller, shallower lake and is stored until power demand is not at its peak. Then the generator turbines are reversed and water is pumped back into the main lake to be used again. Depth of the reregulation pond can vary by 10 feet and its area can vary from more than 1,000 acres to only 60 acres. There are some group tours allowed into the powerhouse itself, but past the lobby, it is not ordinarily open to the public. You can, however, look through the doors and see the generating room beyond.

Back on Old US 411, less than a mile from the road to the powerhouse, cross the Coosawattee River. You can see the 65-foot-high reregulation dam on your left. There are recreation areas on both sides of the Coosawattee here, where the water leaves the reregulation pond. It is a popular fishing spot for catfish, bluegills, striped and hybrid bass, and crappie.

In 1.5 miles, past the waterfowl nesting areas on the left, turn left onto GA 136. The road winds past the privately owned Phoenix Camping Area, and across Talking Rock Creek. At this point, the creek is part of the reregulation impoundment.

Half a mile past Talking Rock Creek, a road on the left winds up Blalock Mountain to the resource manager's office, visitor center, marina, and picnic areas. The marina, the only commercial enterprise on the lake, offers boat rentals and launching as well as cabins.

The visitor center has a spectacular view overlooking the dam, the lake, and the ridges and valleys to the west. At the dam overlook, a historic marker tells about the expedition of Spanish explorer Hernando de Soto, who traveled in this area in 1539–1540. Inside the visitor center is a small museum showing indigenous wildlife as well as artifacts from archaeological digs in the lake area concerning the Indian culture of the region.

Continuing on GA 136, Talking Rock Creek bubbles pleasantly along the right side of the road, through the oak and hickory forest. Do not get too distracted, since GA 136 is a popular truck route, and big rigs are often slowly laboring up the mountain or hurtling down it. Over the ridge of Blalock Mountain and down the other side, turn left onto GA 382. This takes you toward the recreation areas at Harris Branch and Doll Mountain. These Corps of Engineers areas are generally open during the spring, summer, and fall, and closed during the winter.

Seven miles past the Doll Mountain Recreation Area entrance, turn left onto Old Georgia Highway 5 at a T intersection. GA 382 goes right. You then almost immediately come upon a pair of pretty ponds on either side of the road. You have so far seen these ponds and the reregulation impoundment, but unless you have driven into the visitor center area or one of the recreation areas, you will circle the entire 3,200-acre, 11-mile-long Carters Lake and never see Carters Lake itself. From the highways circling the lake, the view of it is hidden by the forested hillsides.

As you return to Ellijay, you once again cross the Coosawattee River. The community uses the floodplain of this river as a fairground, horse arena, ballfields, and parkland. At the junction with US 76, turn right to return to the Zell Miller Mountain Parkway.

Drive 9: Gold Rush

Dahlonega to Vogel State Park to Cleveland

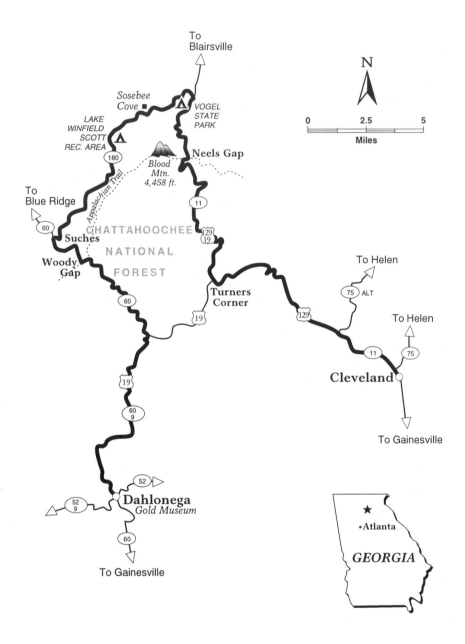

9

Gold Rush

Dahlonega to Vogel State Park to Cleveland

General description: This drive covers about 50 miles; it explores the history of gold in Georgia, the heart of the southern Blue Ridge, and another type of gold in the famous Cabbage Patch Dolls at Babyland General Hospital in Cleveland.

Special attractions: Dahlonega's Gold Museum and operating mines; North Georgia College Campus with the gold-leaf-covered spire of Price Memorial Building; North Georgia Mountains and their glorious seasonal changes including spring, summer, and fall wildflowers, fall leaf color, winter snows, and open hardwood forests; cascading mountain trout streams; warmwater lakes and ponds. Chattahoochee National Forest Recreation Areas have camping, hiking, fishing, and other outdoor activities; Vogel State Park has camping, cottages, hiking, fishing, nature walks, and more. Hunting in the national forest and wildlife management areas is available in season. Babyland General Hospital is where the popular Cabbage Patch dolls are "born."

Location: Northeast Georgia.

Drive route numbers: Georgia Highways 60 and 180, and U.S. Highways 19 and 129.

Travel season: All seasons. Spring, summer, and fall are most popular, and the highways become very crowded during the peak of fall leaf color. Although it snows every year, the roads are open year-round, except during unusually heavy snows.

Camping: USDA Forest Service recreation areas have managed campsites, which close during the winter. Vogel State Park is open year-round with excellent camping and cottage facilities. Most of the campsites on national forest and state park areas have RV hookups. Several private camping areas accommodate camping trailers and other types of RVs. Primitive camping is permitted in much of Chattahoochee National Forest.

Services: Restaurant and motel/hotel accommodations are available in Dahlonega and Cleveland, as well as nearby towns such as Blairsville and Helen. Two restaurants are notable: Smith House in Dahlonega and Ma Gooch's in Cleveland. Both have home-style cooking.

Nearby attractions: Nottely and Chatuge lakes, parts of the Tennessee Valley hydropower system; Blairsville, Young Harris, and Hiawassee, mountain towns with fine gift shops, mountain fairs, and crafts; and the Bavarian-style resort town of Helen.

The drive

This is one of the most varied drives in the state, and encompasses the history of the first gold rush in the United States. It also visits the attractive campus of North Georgia College with its outstanding military program. It passes through the heart of the North Georgia Mountains, with hikes that lead to the Appalachian Trail and the highest point along that trail in Georgia, Blood Mountain. There are three Chattahoochee National Forest recreation sites with camping, hiking trails, and a beautiful fishing lake. Vogel State Park, one of the oldest in the state park system, is beautifully maintained and has excellent play areas for children, several hiking trails, and a pretty lake for fishing and wildlife watching. The drive ends in historic Cleveland at the home of the famous Cabbage Patch dolls.

The drive begins in Dahlonega, the center of America's first gold rush. Gold was discovered in the Georgia mountains in 1828 and at the peak of the rush, $35 million worth of the precious metal was extracted from mines in this district. The Gold Museum, a state historic site, is in the old Lumpkin County courthouse. You can sit down to a movie describing the history of gold in the area or you can just browse the fine displays and collection of gold-mining apparatus. This museum is well worth the time spent on a visit, and is open every day all year except Thanksgiving, Christmas, and New Year's Day.

The Dahlonega town square is ringed with gift shops and food vendors. Only a block from the town square is the Smith House, a famous country-style restaurant.

The North Georgia College campus is west of the town square on Georgia Highway 52 only a few blocks away. The centerpiece of the campus is Price Memorial Building, with its gold leaf spire. Dahlonega gold was applied in 1973 on the one-hundredth anniversary of the college. This building stands on the site of a U. S. Mint, which produced gold coins from 1837 to 1861. There are several gold-mining operations within a few miles of the square, offering tours and the opportunity to pan for gold and keep what you find.

Leaving the Dahlonega square, go east on GA 60/52 and US 19, then turn left at the traffic light on GA 60/US 19. This road winds through the foothills, through a residential section, and on to the beginning of the mountains. Very shortly you will notice many of the trees on both sides of the road broken or bent over in the same direction, the result of a tornado in 1994. The damaged hardwood and pine trees will remain for several years. At 3 miles, you pass Wahsega Road, which leads to Camp Frank Merrill, the principal training site for U.S. Army Rangers and Special Forces. In another 0.5 mile you cross Yahoola Creek, famous for its production of gold. Several

*The Old Lumpkin County Court House is now the
Gold Museum Historic Site in Dahlonega.*

mines were established in this watershed during the height of the gold rush.

At 5 miles, you come to the north end of the US 19/GA 60 Bypass; proceed on toward Suches. The long, low, drab buildings seen on some of the farms are chicken houses. Raising fryer/broiler chickens is one of the major farming activities in north Georgia. One of the landmarks on this highway is a junk store with hundreds of automobile hubcaps. This store is on the left, at about 6 miles.

The road travels on either side of the ridge that ends at the junction of US 19 and GA 60. This is the beginning of the mountains at Stonepile Gap. It is the historic site of the grave of the Cherokee Indian princess, Trahlyta. The rockpile here is the result of a custom of both Indians and whites who dropped stones as they passed for good fortune. This gap is also known as Buffalo Nut Gap.

Stay on GA 60; US 19 turns to the right and leads to Turners Corner and U.S. Highway 129. GA 60 begins a steady climb into the Chattahoochee National Forest and Woody Gap, where the highway crosses the Appalachian Trail.

In spring and summer, the roadsides on the way up are resplendent in wildflowers. In the fall, the mixed hardwood forest is ablaze in reds, yellows, browns, and greens. In winter, with the leaves off the trees, the panorama of surrounding mountains is much more visible. The evergreen shrubs along the road are mountain laurel and rhododendron. The laurel blooms in late April and May. There are two species of rhododendron here: the Catawba rhododendron, which blooms in May and thrives on the drier mountain slopes, and rosebay rhododendron, sometimes called great white rhododendron, which blooms later, from June through July depending on the elevation. Rosebay rhododendron occurs mainly along stream banks and in moist ravines.

On the right, about 2 miles from Stonepile Gap, is a high rock bluff used frequently by rock climbers, especially students in training from North Georgia College and individuals affiliated with outdoor shops in the state. Trees have been cleared from the roadside on the left for vistas of surrounding mountains.

Dockery Lake Road is 2 miles farther. It turns off to the right and leads to the Forest Service's Dockery Lake Recreation Site. Camping, hiking, fishing, and other outdoor activities are available here. A short distance from this road is the Chestatee Overlook. Parking here, you have a better view of the mountains.

At Woody Gap (elevation 3,160 feet), you leave Lumpkin County and enter Union County. The Appalachian Trail crosses here. The trail's southern end at Springer Mountain is 20 miles to the left. The northern end of this trail is at Mount Katahdin in Maine, 2,138 miles to the right. This ridge line is also the divide between the Tennessee River and Etowah River drainages. Woody Gap was named for Arthur Woody, an early forest ranger who worked in the area from 1911 to 1945.

You may encounter dense fog traveling this road in winter and early spring. Although snow is not unusual in winter, this road is seldom closed.

The road now drops down about a thousand feet into the small community of Suches. A single white building on the left, the country store and antique shop, tells you where you are. In about 1 mile, Georgia Highway 180 turns to the right. Just before this intersection is the hostel and campground known as T.W.O. (Two Wheels Only), operated for the many motorcycle riders who enjoy traveling the serpentine mountain roads.

Turn right on GA 180 into a lush valley of small farms and open picturesque pastures. These farms are completely surrounded by the national forest.

In about 4 miles, you come to the entrance to another USDA Forest Service recreation area. This one is named for the pretty Lake Winfield Scott, formed by a dam on the headwaters of Cooper Creek. From this excellent campground, two trails lead to the Appalachian Trail and to Blood Mountain, Georgia's highest point on the long trail. This recreation area includes fishing, swimming, and picnicking, among other activities. It is a good place for spring and summer wildflowers, birding, and wildlife watching.

As you leave the recreation area, you will cross the bridge at the dam impounding the lake. You may see small yellow signs fastened to trees along the left side of GA 180. This is the boundary of the Cooper Creek Wildlife Management Area, which is managed cooperatively by the Georgia Wildlife Resources Division and the USDA Forest Service. In about 3 miles you cross Wolf Pen Gap. The unpaved road to the left is Duncan Ridge Road or Forest Road 39. It goes to the Forest Service's Cooper Creek and Mulky recreation areas. Two well-known hiking trails, Duncan Ridge Trail and the Coosa Backcountry Trail out of Vogel State Park, cross the road in this gap.

The next point of interest is less than a mile. This is Sosebee Cove Scenic Area. The parking area will accommodate only about three cars parallel to the road. A short hiking trail wanders into an excellent stand of second-growth hardwoods, especially yellow poplar trees, and an outstanding array of spring wildflowers including jack-in-the-pulpits, hepaticas, Solomon's-seals, several species of trilliums, and many more. Sosebee Cove Scenic Area is another memorial to Arthur Woody.

From the scenic area, the winding mountain road continues for about 3 miles to US 19/129 and Vogel State Park. To reach the entrance for the park you turn right on US 129 and go about 0.4 mile.

Vogel State Park is one of the oldest and most scenic state parks in Georgia. Wolf Creek flows through the park and is impounded to form picturesque Trahlyta Lake, with a swimming beach, good fishing, and excellent wildlife watching. Cottages and tent and RV camping are available with pleasant playground facilities for children. Four hiking trails range from the

The Sosebee Cove Scenic Area, noted for wildflower display.

short walk around the lake to the 12.7-mile Coosa Backcountry Trail for which a (free) permit is required.

Leaving Vogel Park, turn right on US 19/129 and begin the climb up to Neals Gap. In about 2 miles is the entrance to Byron Reece Memorial parking area. This area is for those planning to hike to Blood Mountain on the Appalachian Trail or other nearby trails. Less than 0.5 mile farther, you come to Neals Gap (elevation 3,125 feet), another crossing of the Appalachian Trail. Walasi Yi Center, a privately operated store with a great collection of hiking/outdoor activity books and equipment is in this gap. Snack food is also available.

From Neals Gap, the road winds and is relatively steep in places for a U.S. highway. There are several turnouts along the way for better vistas of the mountains. About 4 miles from the gap, you come to the entrance to the Forest Service's DeSoto Falls Recreation Area. Tent and RV camping is available. Hiking trails, trout fishing in Frog Creek, scenic waterfalls, and a great variety of wildflowers are some of the features of this area.

In another 4 miles you come to Turners Corner, where US 19 turns to the right. At this junction you can return to Stonepile Gap and on .to Dahlonega, closing a loop and making an alternate drive. The planned drive continues south on US 129 for 11 miles to Cleveland. You are now out of the national forest and back in the foothills where there are small farms and residences along the road, and several private campgrounds along the way. Pass Georgia Highway 75 Alternate that goes to Helen.

In Cleveland, pass several restaurants and motels, go around the courthouse square, and continue on US 129 South. This drive ends a couple blocks from the square at Babyland General Hospital where the famous Cabbage Patch Kids, soft sculptured dolls, came into being through the creativity and entrepreneurship of Xavier Roberts. Visiting hours are from 9 a.m. to 5 p.m., except Sunday when the hours are 10 a.m. to 5 p.m. This is an interesting stop for both young and old.

10

Helen to Brasstown Bald Loop

General description: This 50-mile drive is a typical north Georgia mountain drive that encompasses both the flavor of the Bavarian-style village of Helen and the natural beauty of the mountains in the Chattahoochee National Forest. The apex is at Brasstown Bald, Georgia's highest point, with the return over the Russell Scenic Highway.

Special attractions: The town of Helen and its many gift and craft shops; Brasstown Bald, Georgia's highest point; Richard B. Russell Scenic Highway; grand fall colors and spring and summer flowers; Unicoi State Park and Anna Ruby Falls Scenic Area; Andrews Cove Recreation Area; excellent hiking trails; and trout fishing and hunting in season on the Chattahoochee National Forest and state wildlife management areas.

Location: Northeast Georgia mountains.

Drive route numbers: Georgia Highways 75/17, 356, 180, 348 (Richard B. Russell Scenic Highway) and 75 Alternate.

Travel season: This is a drive that has special attractions at any season. The roads are crowded during the height of fall leaf color. Spring and summer are ideal times for flowering plants. Hiking weather occurs throughout the year; however, some roads and trails may be temporarily closed during brief periods of heavy snow.

Camping: Camping is available, except during the winter months, in the Forest Service campground at Andrews Cove Recreation Area. Unicoi State Park and Lodge has excellent camping facilities and a 100-room lodge and restaurant. Private campgrounds, including Brasstown Village Resort, are near the surrounding towns. Primitive camping is permitted in some areas of the national forest.

Services: Excellent restaurants, motels, and hotels in Helen, Hiawassee, and Blairsville. Unicoi State Park and Lodge has a buffet-style restaurant and rooms and cottages. Cabins are available at Brasstown Village Resort.

Nearby attractions: Anna Ruby Falls Recreation Area near Unicoi State Park; Hiawassee and the Georgia Mountain Fair; Track Rock Archaeological Area; and many side trips into Chattahoochee National Forest and mountain towns, including Cleveland and its Babyland General Hospital.

 The drive

The town of Helen has been transformed from a small, sleepy mountain village to a bustling Bavarian-style tourist town with many gift shops,

Drive 10: Helen to Brasstown Bald Loop

Brasstown Bald
4,788 ft.

To Hiawassee

CHATTAHOOCHEE   NATIONAL   FOREST

Jacks
Gap   180

Brasstown
Village

To Blairsville

180

129

180

129

CHATTAHOOCHEE
NATIONAL FOREST

Unicoi
Gap

Andrews
Cove

Appalachian Trail

Richard B. Russell

Chattahoochee River

75
17

Anna Ruby
Falls

UNICOI
STATE PARK

Hog Pen
Gap

Scenic Highway

Robertstown

Helen

RAVEN CLIFFS
WILDERNESS AREA

Dukes
Creek
Falls

75   ALT

Dukes Creek

To
Clarkesville

17

SMITHGALL WOOD
WILDLIFE MANAGEMENT AREA

N

Atlanta

GEORGIA

75   ALT

To
Cleveland

75

To
Cleveland

0   2.5   5

Miles

motels and hotels, restaurants, and amusements. The drive begins here and travels north on Georgia Highway 17/75. Drive 2 miles along the Chattahoochee River, which flows right through Helen and the next community, Robertstown. Here you turn right on Georgia Highway 356 and go about 2 miles to Unicoi State Park. Forest Road 242 is on the left just before you cross the dam. Take this road to Anna Ruby Falls parking area and visitor center. A 0.4-mile paved trail leads to the falls. Return to GA 356. If you wish to visit Unicoi State Park, turn to the left and cross the dam of the picturesque lake. About 100 yards farther, the road to the park's campground and cabins turns to the left and the road to the lodge and restaurant turns to the right. The lodge and conference center houses one the finest collections of handmade quilts in the country.

Backtrack down GA 356 to Robertstown and turn right on GA 17/75. GA 75 Alternate turns to the left and crosses the Chattahoochee River. The loop drive will come back to this point. Continue on GA 17/75, enter Chattahoochee National Forest, and begin a steady climb into the mountains.

In about 1.5 miles, pass Forest Road 79. This unpaved road leads to Indian Grave Gap, crosses the Appalachian Trail, becomes Forest Road 283, descends to the parking area for High Shoals Falls Scenic Area, fords the Hiwassee River and comes back out on Georgia 17/75 across the mountain. This is an interesting drive, but is not recommended for vehicles with low road clearance because it is necessary to ford the stream; depending on weather conditions, it may be difficult for other than four-wheel-drive vehicles.

Passing by the forest road you continue for another 3 miles, where you come to the entrance to Andrews Cove Recreation Area. This is a pleasant campground with tent and RV campsites; a hiking path that accesses the Appalachian Trail begins here. This is a typical hardwood cove. Dogwoods, silverbells, azaleas, and yellow poplar bloom in the spring, followed later by rhododendrons and mountain laurels.

Continuing up the mountain about 3 miles brings you to Unicoi Gap (elevation 2,949 feet). This is the watershed divide between the Chattahoochee River valley that extends south to Florida, and the Tennessee River valley to the north that empties into the Mississippi River. The Appalachian Trail is routed through this gap toward Tray Mountain and North Carolina. On the way up to the gap and down the north side there are occasional turnouts where trees have been cleared for better views of the mountains.

The winding mountain road drops down the north slope of Blue Mountain into the Hiwassee River valley. In about 3.5 miles you come to GA 180. Turn left toward Brasstown Bald. In about 2 miles you pass the sign and entrance to the privately operated Brasstown Village Resort. This area was originally developed as a Civilian Conservation Corps work camp in the 1930s, and later used as a YMCA summer camp. There are cabins, tent and RV campsites, waterfalls, hiking trails, and trout fishing.

The next point of interest comes in about 3 miles, where GA 180 Spur turns to the right at Jacks Gap. From here, climb about 1,500 feet in 3 miles to Brasstown Bald parking area. This is a very steep drive. Turnouts are provided for views of surrounding mountains or, if necessary, for cooling engines. The Chattahoochee/Oconee Heritage Association operates a gift shop at the parking area. A parking fee is required.

An outstanding visitor center is on the summit of Brasstown Bald. You can walk to the visitor center along a 0.5-mile trail that climbs another 500 feet, or ride a shuttle bus. The visitor center is open seven days a week from late May through October. An observation deck provides a 360-degree view of the North Georgia Mountains and into Tennessee and North Carolina. The center has a video program and educational displays of mountain plants, animals, and people, including their history. People requiring a wheelchair can request access to the visitor center.

High gaps where roads cross the mountain, and high points like this one at Brasstown Bald, are ideal places for birders to watch and listen for migrating songbirds and raptors. Many songbirds pass by these areas on their way north in spring. In the fall, you will often see migrating hawks on their southbound journeys.

From the parking area, several interesting hiking trails pass through tunnels of rhododendron and mountain laurel. Spring flowers are particularly abundant around the parking area and along the trails. In earliest spring, patches of bluets, robin plantains, Solomon's-seals, toothworts, trilliums, pink lady's-slippers, and others are in bloom. Later, mountain laurel blooms; in June, the Catawba rhododendrons come into flower.

Take it easy down the steep grade back to GA 180, and turn right and drive about 7 miles to GA 348, the Richard B. Russell Scenic Highway. On the way, you leave the national forest for a few miles and pass through quiet, picturesque mountain farm land. These are private in-holdings inside the forest boundary, with pastoral scenes of cattle feeding in hillside pastures, and fields of corn and cabbage with vegetable gardens near the homes.

Track Rock Road intersection is along the way; it leads to the Track Rock Archaeological Area, a site with ancient Indian petroglyphs. The carvings from which the mountain gap receives its name resemble animal tracks and other impressions.

Continue on GA 180 to GA 348, turn left, and continue through more private land. This area is known as Choestoe, pronounced "cho-ess-TOE-ee," an Indian word meaning "dancing rabbit." This was the home of celebrated

Catawba rhododendron in bloom at Brasstown Bald.

mountain poet Herbert Byron Reese. "The Reach of Song," a musical play inspired by Reese's life, is performed each summer in nearby Hiawassee.

You will enter the national forest again and begin the climb to 3,480-foot-high Hog Pen Gap. The sourwood trees bloom in the summer, and bees collecting nectar from these flowers produce delicious sourwood honey.

From GA 180 to Hog Pen is about 7 miles. You pass a lesser gap called Tesnatee Gap where the old Logan Turnpike crossed the mountain. A short trail here leads to the Appalachian Trail. In another 0.5 mile, you come to Hog Pen Gap. Markers and interpretive signs tell of the Appalachian Trail and Benton MacKaye, the New England forester who originally planned this long Georgia-to-Maine hiking trail. In spring, a colony of yellow lady's-slipper orchids bloom along the trail to the southeast.

As you leave the gap and continue south down the mountain, the Raven Cliff Scenic Area and Raven Cliff Wilderness Area are on the right. Raven Cliff Falls Trail provides walking access into this area. In about 5.5 miles you come to the Duke Creek Falls Recreation Area. In the parking area is a restroom and the beginning of a paved, barrier-free trail that leads to a large wooden platform providing a good view of the falls. The falls is formed by Davis Creek, a tributary to Dukes Creek. From the platform, a hiking trail leads a mile down the steep-sided valley to Dukes Creek. The many switchbacks in the trail keep the grade from being too steep. Dukes Creek supports a fine wild trout population.

Back on the Scenic Highway it is about 2 miles to GA 75 Alt. The entrance to the Dukes Creek/Smithgall Woods Conservation Area is on the right. This unique area is managed by the Natural Resources Department and includes a trophy trout stream, carefully managed hunting, an environmental education program and more.

Turn left on GA 75 Alt., travel about 2 miles to the intersection with GA 17/75, and the loop drive is closed. A right turn takes you back to Helen.

11

Georgia Highway 197

Clarkesville to Tallulah Gorge

General description: A drive through the upper foothills of North Georgia, through the pleasant town of Clarkesville, following the Soquee River to Burton Lake, and down the Tallulah River Valley and Georgia Power Company reservoirs to the dramatic Tallulah Gorge State Park.

Special attractions: Although small, the Soquee River is a pretty stream in a narrow, heavily forested valley. The Mark of the Potter shop is well worth the stop to see pottery being made and to feed the large trout in the Soquee River beside the shop. The Georgia Power Company dams and reservoirs on the Tallulah River and the breathtaking Tallulah Gorge, waterfalls, and hiking trails add greatly to this drive.

Location: Northeast Georgia foothills lying abreast of the higher mountains.

Drive route numbers: Georgia Highways 365 and 197; Burton Dam Road; Old U.S. Highway 441; and the wide four-lane U.S. Highway 441.

Travel season: This drive is interesting throughout the year. Only after rare heavy snowfalls is the road impassable. Wildflowers in spring and summer and exceptional fall leaf color make this a choice drive. Winter is especially nice; with the leaves off the trees, you have a much better view of the surrounding mountains.

Camping: The USDA Forest Service Rabun Beach Recreation Area has a well-managed campground for tent and RV camping. At Tallulah Gorge State Park's Terrora Park, there are 50 tent and trailer sites. There is a fee for camping in these sites. Primitive camping is permitted on the Chattahoochee National Forest. Moccasin Creek State Park has a tent and trailer campground.

Services: Lodging and food are available in and around Clarkesville. The Batesville General Store serves fresh cinnamon rolls and biscuits. Food and gas are available at the intersection of GA 197 and Burton Dam Road. Quaint, rustic Rabun Hotel is on the Burton Dam Road. Only about 15 miles off the drive, the towns of Helen and Clayton offer additional opportunities for food, lodging, and gas.

Nearby attractions: The Alpine-style village of Helen and Unicoi State Park; Clayton and Black Rock Mountain State Park; Moccasin Creek State Park with trout fishing for children and senior citizens only; Lake Burton State Fish Hatchery; Chattooga River with whitewater rafting, hiking trails and fishing; and the Chattahoochee National Forest with camping and other outdoor activities at several nearby recreation areas.

Drive 11: Georgia Highway 197
Clarkesville to Tallulah Gorge

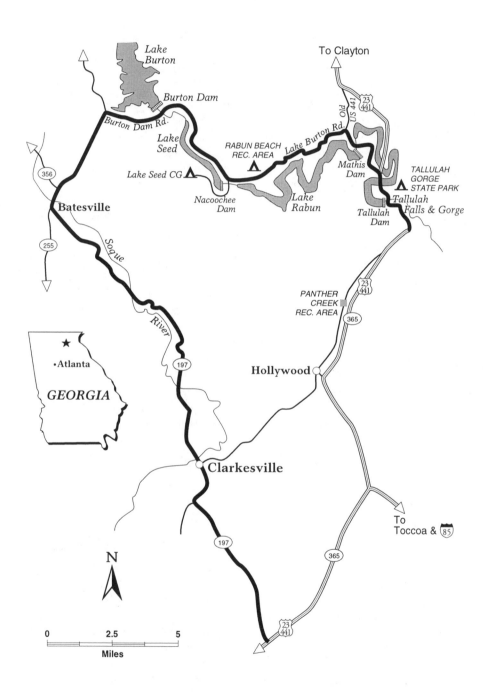

Lake Burton

To Clayton

Burton Dam

Burton Dam Rd.

Lake Seed

RABUN BEACH REC. AREA

Lake Burton Rd.

Old US 441

23 441

356

Lake Seed CG

Nacoochee Dam

Lake Rabun

Mathis Dam

TALLULAH GORGE STATE PARK

Tallulah Falls & Gorge

Batesville

255

Sogue

River

Tallulah Dam

197

PANTHER CREEK REC. AREA

23 441

365

★

•Atlanta

GEORGIA

Hollywood

Clarkesville

To Toccoa & 85

197

365

N

23 441

0   2.5   5
Miles

 # The drive

Begin this drive at the intersection of Georgia Highway 197 with GA 365 and U.S. Highway 441/23, the four-lane divided highway to northeast Georgia. Traveling north on GA 197 leads you to Clarkesville in about 4 miles. On the way, you pass through rolling foothills and pastoral scenes. Most of the agriculture is now devoted to cattle and poultry farms and a few apple orchards. The poultry farms are characterized by long, low buildings where the chickens are raised prior to shipment throughout the United States.

The business center of Clarkesville has a number of nice shops. The historical buildings and other features are described in Drive 13, the Toccoa Loop. GA 197 goes around the square, makes a right turn, then turns to the left after a block, and leaves town crossing the Soquee (pronounced "so-KWEE") River bridge. In a short distance you pass by the USDA Forest Service Chattooga Ranger District office on the right. In about a mile you pass North Georgia Vocational School, a landmark of early rural education.

As you leave the residential area north of Clarkesville, you begin to get views of the North Georgia mountains, then drop down into the Soquee River Valley and cross the river again. GA 197 follows the Soquee into Chattahoochee National Forest.

During the early spring, expect to see redbud and dogwood trees make their show along the roadway. They will be followed by flame azaleas blooming in the mixed hardwood forest before the leaves completely shade the forest floor. Along the road banks in April and May, you might see patches of blue birdfoot violets. In autumn, this is a good drive for fall leaf color.

This two-lane macadam road crosses the Soquee River four times; at times, the river runs beside the road. At one point, marked with a "DIP" sign, a small feeder creek runs across the highway. This is a winding road offering little opportunity to pass vehicles ahead of you, so just relax and enjoy the scenery.

Although this drive is inside the boundary of the Chattahoochee National Forest, most of the route passes through private land in small farms and widely spaced residences. You will see the long, low buildings of the poultry farms, and beef cattle grazing on hillside pastures. About 8 miles from Clarkesville, the Soquee River is along the left side of the road, and you are in the national forest proper. Cross the river again, and in about 0.5 mile, pass Watts Mill Road on the right. In less than 0.5 mile you come to The Mark of the Potter, a pottery and gift shop located in an old grist mill. There is gravel roadside parking. At this point, the Soquee River supports trout; to prove it, all you have to do is obtain some food from the gift shop, toss it into the stream, and watch enormous trout feed. You guessed it! Fishing is not allowed in this private section of the stream. However, fishing is permitted nearby at the Riverside Trout Pond and Trophy Stream, where you can fish for large trout. Guide service is available.

The Mark of the Potter is the oldest craft shop in northeast Georgia. Often, there are potters at work at the wheels, shaping clay into decorative and useful items. The gift shop carries the work of thirty local potters, glass-blowers, and jewelers. The grist mill grinds corn meal regularly. Other craft shops are along the road.

In about 1.5 miles you come to Georgia Highway 255 on the left. at the community of Batesville. This intersection has the Batesville General Store,

A bluff with falls in Tallulah Gorge.

which serves biscuits and fresh cinnamon rolls, and The Wood Duck Shop, with museum-quality wildlife carvings.

A mile later you pass Georgia Highway 356, which goes to Unicoi State Park and Helen. Leave the Soquee River Valley and continue on GA 197. The next 4 miles takes you through typical mountain farming area interspersed with clusters of shops selling a variety of mountain crafts and antiques. Then, you reach the intersection with Burton Dam Rd., which has a service station, gift shops and restaurants. Turn right on Burton Dam Rd. and enter the Tallulah River valley. The Georgia Power Company has six dams that impound lakes in this scenic valley. This drive will pass four of them.

Picturesque Lake Burton is on the left, surrounded by mountains in the distance and with private homes lining its shore. From here the road is very steep going down into the Tallulah River valley. Those driving RVs or pulling trailers are advised to shift to a lower gear. You reach the bottom of the valley and cross the Tallulah River about 1.5 miles from the intersection. Burton Dam is to the left, upstream. To the downstream side is the head of Lake Seed. Charlie Mountain Road turns off to the left about 0.5 mile from the bridge. Continue straight on Burton Dam Rd., following the narrow valley, with the lake visible from time to time on the right through the heavy forest cover. The road is now called Lake Rabun Road. In about 3 miles you pass the only public boat-launching ramp on Lake Seed.

Look for azaleas, rhododendron, and mountain laurel to be blooming from late April through May. Because of the great variety of hardwood trees on the mountains, fall leaf color can be spectacular in this valley. These lakes support a warmwater fishery for bass, bluegill, crappie, and even an occasional walleye and hybrid bass (white bass/striped bass cross).

About a mile farther, the road on the right takes you to Glenn Ella Springs and the Lake Seed Campground. Glen Ella is a refurbished resort hotel dating to the turn of the century, when Tallulah Falls drew visitors from around the world. The wilderness campground at Seed Lake features a sandy beach, picnic area, and latrines, but no drinking water is available.

Next downstream is Lake Rabun, and in about 1 mile you come to the first entrance to the Forest Service's Rabun Beach Recreation Area on the left. The second entrance is not quite 1 mile farther. Tent, trailer, and RV camping is available in a pleasant shaded setting. At the upper end of the campground is a hiking trail along Joe Creek to Angel and Panther falls. Between the two entrances to the Rabun Beach area is the sign for Minnehaha Trail and Falls. In about 0.5 mile, Lake Rabun is in view again along with elaborate boat docks and cottages. You pass the marina and cluster of residences, Lake Rabun Hotel, other cottages, and inns, which are only open during the warm weather tourist season. In about 2 more miles, you reach the intersection with Old U.S. Highway 441. Turn right and immediately

Mark of the Potter Mill and craft shop on Soquee River, home to very large trout.

cross the Tallulah River below Mathis Dam, which impounds Lake Rabun. Follow this road for 2.5 miles to the new US 441/23. Turn right, and in about 1 mile you will see the sign for Tallulah Gorge State Park. At the time of this writing, the state park is adding a visitor center and environmental education program. The Georgia Power Company's Terrora Visitor Center is on the right just before you cross the Tallulah River again, above the falls and gorge.

The drive ends here at Tallulah Gorge, which is nearly 1,000 feet deep—a dramatic natural area with grand views and unique natural history. Several endangered plants and rare animals are found here and nowhere else. It is the oldest natural gorge in the United States and second in depth only to the Grand Canyon in Arizona. The old town of Tallulah Falls is rich in history from the days before the river was dammed. Visitors from around the world came to marvel at the thundering series of cascades that once dropped the Tallulah River over 1,000 feet in 3 miles. That roaring torrent was silenced with the construction of Tallulah Dam and Power Station, considered one of the great engineering achievements of its day.

12

Rabun County Loop
Clayton to Dillard to Rabun Bald

General description: This 42-mile loop on winding paved and unpaved roads dips in and out of North Carolina. You drive through the mountain towns of Clayton, Dillard, and Sky Valley to Georgia's second highest mountain, Rabun Bald, and back down to the West Fork of the Chattooga River and back to Clayton. The paved roads are winding, steep in places, and two lanes except for U.S. Highway 441/23 from Clayton to Dillard. The unpaved Forest Roads 7 and 86 are occasionally one lane.

Special attractions: The drive leads to interesting hiking trails, trout streams, and lush forests. Wildflowers abound, and birding is very good, especially for warblers, during spring and fall migration. Fall leaf color is especially grand on the drive because of the great variety of deciduous trees. The towns have fine craft and gift shops. Deer, turkey, black bear, squirrels, and other wildlife abound in the forest but are infrequently seen because of the dense foliage. A hiking trail leads to Rabun Bald, the second highest mountain in the state at 4,696 feet. Walkers can travel the famed Bartram Trail. The West Fork of the Chattooga River and Holcomb Creek are popular trout-fishing streams. The Warwoman Wildlife Management Area is encircled by the drive. Managed big- and small-game hunting is permitted here during special seasons.

Location: Northeast corner of the state.

Drive route numbers: U.S. Highway 441/23, Georgia Highway 246, Mud Creek Road, Forest Roads 7 and 86 (Hales Ridge and Overflow Creek roads, respectively), and Warwoman Road.

Travel season: An all-season drive with special attractions year-round. Spring and summer offer flowering herbs, shrubs, and trees; fall is the time for splendid leaf color. Winter affords the best mountain views when the trees are bare. During winter there may be days of heavy snow, when unpaved Forest Service roads are closed or passable only with four-wheel-drive vehicles. The paved road from Dillard to Sky Valley is steep and winding, and may also be impassable for short periods during snow or ice conditions.

Camping: Primitive camping in Chattahoochee National Forest. One camping area on Forest Road 86 has a comfort station. Black Rock Mountain State Park has excellent camping facilities for RVs and tents. Moccasin Creek State Park has camping, too.

Services: Gas, fine motels, and restaurants are available in Clayton and

Drive: 12 Rabun County Loop
Clayton to Dillard to Rabun Bald

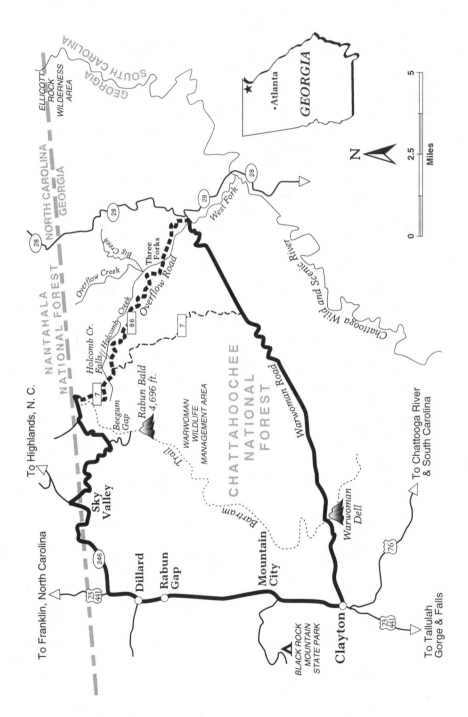

Dillard. The Dillard House is famous for food and service. The USDA Forest Service Tallulah Ranger District Office is in Clayton on US 441. There you can get information on camping, hiking, and other forest uses.

Nearby attractions: Black Rock Mountain State Park; Tallulah Gorge State Park; Chattooga Wild and Scenic River; Highlands, North Carolina; Lake Burton; Moccasin Creek State Park and Moccasin Creek State Trout Hatchery; and many miles of fine trout fishing streams.

 The drive

This loop drive through the peaks of the Blue Ridge mountains touches one of the most popular tourist areas of the state. Rabun County is the northeasternmost county in the state, and for over a century, families escaping summer's heat have made these highlands their summer retreat. The local claim that this is "where spring spends the summer."

First settled just after the American Revolution, it is a land of high, rounded mountains and fertile valleys. From here flow headwater streams for the Savannah and the Tennessee rivers. Adventurers can find whitewater thrills to the east on the Chattooga River, where outfitters offer daily trips through rapids with names like Bull Sluice, Corkscrew, and Sockemdog. Hikers and backpackers can follow the Bartram Trail over the mountain peaks. For those who seek relaxation, to the west is Lake Burton, the shores of which are lined with vacation cottages and the waters offer skiing, fishing, and cruising. South is Tallulah Falls, with spectacular views of the oldest natural river gorge in the United States. North is Highlands, North Carolina, with upscale shopping and golfing. At the center of it all is Clayton, Mountain City, and Dillard.

Beginning and ending in Clayton, this loop drive goes north through Mountain City and Dillard, then east, nicking the edge of North Carolina. It passes Sky Valley, then heads southeast along Forest Service roads through Chattahoochee National Forest. It then passes 4,696-foot-high Rabun Bald and down along streams forming the West Fork, then leads west along the Warwoman Valley back to Clayton. Though under 40 miles long, the trip will take several hours. Much of it is on dirt and gravel forest roads, and most of it is winding, with many sharp curves. Autos with extremely low ground clearance and extra-large recreational vehicles may have problems negotiating these roads.

The drive begins at the intersection of Warwoman Road with US 441 in Clayton. Go north on US 441. You are driving alongside Stekoa Creek, with Black Rock Mountain to the left. From Mountain City, Black Rock Road leads left 2 miles to Black Rock Mountain State Park, which offers camping, cabins, picnic facilities, and panoramic views of the area. As US 441 tops a small rise in the road just north of Mountain City, you cross the Tennessee Valley Divide. This is the eastern continental divide. Behind you, water runs into the Savannah River drainage and eventually into the Atlantic Ocean. In front of you, the water runs into the Tennessee River drainage, which flows into the Mississippi River and eventually into the Gulf of Mexico.

As you drive through the Nacoochee Valley, you'll see fields of produce, primarily to your right. Coleslaw lovers will no doubt be impressed by the fact that this is one of the largest cabbage-producing areas in the state. The open-sided buildings to your right are packing sheds where cabbage and other vegetables are prepared for market when they are harvested in the summer. On the left are the grounds and campus of Rabun Gap Nacoochee School. It was founded in 1903, and originally offered entire families a way to work their way through school.

Across the fields to your right is the Dillard House, one of the older hostelries in the valley. It is famous for its food, served family-style. The town of Dillard has a number of crafts and antique stores beckoning to passersby.

Turn right 1 mile north of Dillard on Georgia Highway 246. After crossing the Little Tennessee River, you begin to climb toward Estatoah Falls, where Mud Creek tumbles over the side of Raven Rock.

We are heading up onto the mountains, toward Highlands, North Carolina. This community is a long-time favorite of lowlanders escaping the summer heat and is well worth a visit. We, however, will just nip off a tiny bit of North Carolina before we turn off and enjoy the Georgia portion of the mountains. On your left, where the mountainside has been cut away in road construction, you will see kudzu growing. This Japanese vine was introduced to control erosion, but it spreads so quickly that it became a pest. Groundhogs, however, love it. If you travel this road while the kudzu is dormant in the colder months, you can see groundhog burrows dug in the banks, and occasionally even see a "whistle pig" sunning itself in a burrow entrance.

As the road continues to climb, you can stop and enjoy the view back out over the Nacoochee Valley at a turnout on the right.

About a quarter mile after the road crosses the North Carolina State Line, turn right at Mountain Junction General Store. This is Old Mud Creek Road, and leads to Sky Valley. Started in the 1970s, this resort community boasts Georgia's only ski slopes, plus golfing in the warmer months. The entrance to Sky Valley is to the right.

Continue on Old Mud Creek Road, and about 0.5 mile past Fish Hawk Ford Mountain Fishing School on the left, Old Rabun Bald Road goes to the right. This dirt road runs 0.5 mile to Beegum Gap. From there, a hiking path leads to the top of Rabun Bald, Georgia's second highest peak (Brasstown

View from GA 246 on drive to Sky Valley and Rabun Bald.

Bald in Union County is highest, at 4,784 feet). A stone tower at the summit of Rabun Bald offers a panoramic view from this 4,696-foot elevation.

Old Mud Creek Rd. passes a number of homes, and thickets of mountain laurel and rhododendron put on a beautiful show in season. Mountain laurel blooms first, in late spring, and the rhododendron, a type of mountain azalea, blossoms in July.

Please note: You will pass John Valley Rd. on the right before you get to your next turn. John Valley Rd. is not the road you want to be on; your turn is coming up, at Hale Ridge Road (Forest Road 7) Turn right onto this narrow, gravel road; it is passable for the average family car, but if your car is low to the ground, or if you are in a large recreational vehicle, you probably should turn back here. To the right, you can see the round face of Rabun Bald above you.

Passing a number of vacation homes, you soon plunge into the Chattahoochee National Forest. This is primarily hardwood, mixed with some hemlock and white pines. The woods are thick here, so to actually see the surrounding mountains you should come in the winter when the trees are bare.

About a mile from your turnoff onto Hale Ridge Road, you cross Bartram Trail. This footpath is named for naturalist William Bartram, whose travels through Georgia prior to the Revolutionary War provided some of the first descriptions of the plants and animals of the southeastern United States.

The large oval-leafed shrub at the trail crossing is a rhododendron. A sign tells you that the distance by path to Rabun Bald is 4.2 miles.

You are high in the mountains, winding along this cool, shady road. It's a chance to slow down and enjoy where you are. Two miles past Bartram Trail, you cross Holcomb Creek. This streamlet is one of three creeks that form the West Fork.

A half-mile later, you pick up Forest Road 86 (Overflow Creek Road). Hale Ridge Rd. (FR 7) goes to the right. Continue straight onto FR 86. This road runs along the edge of the Chattooga Wild and Scenic River corridor. Blue blazes painted on trees on the left mark this boundary. In 1974, the U.S. Congress designated this area Wild and Scenic, protecting it from development and restricting access to foot travel. You can see Holcomb Creek, which by now is a much larger stream than the brook you first crossed, off to your left. There are occasionally turnoffs to primitive camping spots along the creek.

A mile past the intersection with Forest Road 868 (Billingsly Creek Road) on the left, you climb to John Teague Gap. To your left, Three Forks Trail leads to the convergence of Holcomb Creek, Overflow Creek, and Big

An old stone marker for the Bartram Trail near Warwoman Road.

Forest Road 86 (Overflow Creek Road) with mountain laurel in bloom.

Creek, where the West Fork is born.

Two and a half miles past John Teague Gap, past Tottery Pole Creek, you get your first look at the West Fork. It is large for a mountain stream and popular with anglers, campers, whitewater rafters, and canoeists. Known as Section 1, the whitewater from here to the Chattooga is milder than that on the more famous Sections 2 and 3 on the Chattooga itself.

As the road levels, there is a developed Forest Service campground on the right. It features comfort stations, but no drinking water.

A mile later, turn right on Warwoman Road. You are back on pavement for the first time in almost 11 miles. The road is practically as winding as the Forest Service roads, but a lot wider and smoother. This road is named for Nancy Hart, heroine of the American Revolution. The Cherokee called her "War Woman."

As you continue along Warwoman Rd., you are following a narrow valley through Cornpen Gap, along Morsingill's Creek, then through Goble Gap to parallel Warwoman Creek. The small farms and homes along of this route are what many people picture when they think of mountain cabins.

This drive has nearly circled the Warwoman Wildlife Management Area. Administered by the Georgia Department of Natural Resources, it is a popular hunting area, as well as being used for other outdoor recreation.

Near Antioch, 2 miles past Earls Ford Road, Black Diamond Road leads to the left and takes you near the site of the Black Diamond Tunnel. In 1854, laborers started drilling a tunnel through Wall Mountain as part of the Black Diamond Railroad. This rail line was to link the port at Charleston with commerce of the Nashville basin in Tennessee. The venture died before the tunnel was finished, so the workmen abandoned their tools and materials in the shaft and left. The Black Diamond Tunnel has mostly filled with water, and the equipment is still there nearly a century and a half later. The site, however, is on private land and is not open to the public. You *can* see a portion of the Black Diamond Railroad, 3.2 miles up Warwoman Road at Warwoman Dell. This picnic area on your left is at the site of an old fish hatchery. A section of the never-finished rail bed is visible from the hillside near the parking area. The Bartram Trail also runs through here, and if you follow it north across the road (carefully!), a short hike takes you to Becky Branch Waterfall.

When you come to the Clayton City limits, stay on Warwoman Rd., which will take you to your starting point at the intersection with US 441.

13

Toccoa Loop

Hollywood, Clarkesville, Cornelia

General description: A loop drive of about 75 miles takes you through the foothills area of northeast Georgia with hills and prominent ridges, some with exposed granite cliffs.

Special attractions: Rural countryside with small farms; Travelers Rest Historic Site; Lake Hartwell; old barns, churches, and church cemeteries; historic colleges; Currahee Mountain; Toccoa Falls; and Toccoa Falls College with its beautiful campus and gift shop. Joseph Habersham historic marker in Clarkesville; interesting shops on the square in Clarkesville; the Big Red Apple and the train station in Cornelia; Mayflower weathervane on the steeple at Piedmont College, a Congregational Christian college. Good view of Currahee Mountain from Georgia Highway105 at Currahee Baptist Church.

Location: Northeast Georgia's upper Piedmont region.

Drive route numbers: Interstate 85; Georgia Highways 320, 63, 17, 123, 105, and 184; and U.S. Highway 441/23.

Travel season: Year-round with fall best for leaf color, and winter for views of mountains and Christmas at Traveler's Rest.

Camping: USDA Forest Service Lake Russell Recreation Area, Fern Springs Recreation Area, and primitive camping in some parts of the Chattahoochee National Forest.

Services: Good restaurants, lodging, and gasoline in the small towns.

Nearby attractions: Tallulah Falls State Park; Tugaloo and Yonah lakes and dams; Hartwell Lake; Lake Russell Recreation Area and Wildlife Management Area; and northeast Georgia mountains.

 The drive

The Cherokees named this drive; in their language, *toccoa* means "beautiful," and can be applied to more than the main town on this route. You will encounter a gracious plenty of beauty in this trip through the upper Piedmont of northeast Georgia. There is also history, outdoor recreation, shopping, and Indian lore.

This is border country. Lake Hartwell east of Toccoa is the boundary of Georgia with South Carolina. East of Clakesville, Cornelia, and Baldwin,

Drive 13: Toccoa Loop
Hollywood, Clarkesville, Cornelia

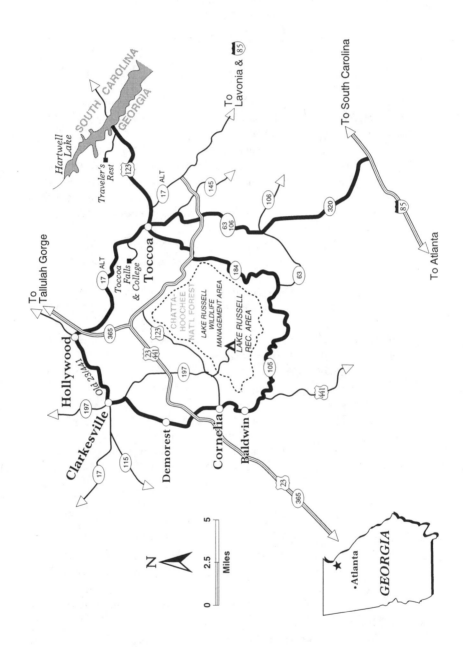

the Bates Line marked the border between the United States and the Cherokee Nation in the early 1800s. Also, U.S. Highway 441 Business through Clarkesville, Cornelia, and Baldwin follows the eighteenth-century demarcation between the Cherokees and the Creek Confederation.

This is a loop drive with two tails hanging out at Toccoa. Tail one is the access route to and from Interstate 85. Tail two is the short trip to the remarkably preserved Travelers Rest Inn. For those wanting a shorter trip, or who wish to simply start at the north part of the loop, it is intersected by Georgia Highway 365, a four-lane extension of Interstate 985 at Gainesville. By starting and finishing the loop at Cornelia or Hollywood, you eliminate driving to Toccoa and back from I-85, a total of about 35 miles.

Anytime of year is fine for this trip, and each season has its charms. However, fall leaf color can be breathtaking. Much of this route is not on the traditional path of the leaf-looking public, so you may enjoy the display without being in a traffic jam the entire way. There is more tourist traffic in the towns on the north part of the drive; consequently, this is where you'll find more tourist accommodations and attractions. Clarkesville in particular has transformed its downtown section into a shopping zone with numerous attractive shops. Demorest and Cornelia, with charms of their own, are also geared to sightseers.

If your interests turn to the natural, the drive is largely in the Chattahoochee National Forest, providing hiking, camping, hunting, and fishing. The Forest Service's Lake Russell Recreation Area near Cornelia is open from Memorial Day to Labor Day, and offers swimming, picnicking, fishing, hiking, and camping. The adjacent Lake Russell Wildlife Management Area also has hiking, primitive camping, and hunting in season. Hartwell Lake is a superb fishing lake with all water sports.

This route is near five other drives in this book: Drives 9, 10, 11, 12, and 14.

The drive begins on Georgia Highway 320 at its junction with Interstate 85. Head north on GA 320. Old farms and fields line the highway, with patches of cut-over timberland.

In 9 miles, pick up Georgia Highways 63 and 106 at the Stephens County Line. Stephens County was established in 1905 and named for Alexander Stephens, vice-president of the Confederate States (see Drive 15). The land has been occupied far longer than the county has existed. The Creeks and Cherokee fought over this territory until both were driven out in the 1830s. There are country churches along the road now, with neat cemeteries and shelters with tables where families in the congregation bring food for traditional "dinner on the grounds."

You will come to Georgia Highway 17, which bypasses Toccoa. Cross it and continue straight on GA 63. Soon you can see Currahee Mountain to the left. Currahee Mountain, from the Cherokee word for "standing alone," is an upthrust granite outcropping. This dramatic peak, 1,874 feet above sea level, is the most striking object on the horizon.

As you come into downtown Toccoa, the Toccoa Casket Company is on the left. They are one of America's largest manufacturers of burial furniture. Toccoa is one of the largest towns in the northeast corner of the state. It is located on a main line of the Norfolk-Southern Railroad, and is served by the Amtrak Crescent passenger train. Once the home to a LeTourneau heavy machinery plant, the town has the look of a small industrial center.

Turn right onto U.S. Highway 123. The Toccoa Welcome Center is on the left in a couple of blocks. It has information on the nearby Stephens County Museum, Henderson Falls Park, and other local attractions. For map buffs, they also have a selection of southeastern and midwestern state roadmaps.

US 123 is an old-fashioned two-lane road leading northeast out of Toccoa to the towns of Westminster, Seneca, and Greenville, South Carolina. About 5 miles from the welcome center, a sign indicates the turnoff to the left for Travelers Rest. Take this road and follow it 0.3 mile over a small arm of Hartwell Lake. The old building on the right at the bend in the road is Travelers Rest, and was built between 1816 and 1825. Located near a ferry (later, a bridge,) across the Tugaloo River, Travelers Rest served as an inn, trading post, and post office. It has not offered overnight accommodations for years, but you can enjoy touring the building and grounds, including a blacksmith shop and weaving looms. Some of the furnishings are original to the building. It is now administered by the Georgia Department of Natural Resources as a State Historic Site. The Christmas program here is particularly popular.

Head back to Toccoa, and turn right onto GA 17 Alternate. Less than 2 miles north of Toccoa you will come to the gates of Toccoa Falls College on the left. Through these gates, follow the signs for a mile to reach Toccoa Falls. Local people are proud to point out that this 186-foot waterfall is 19 feet higher than Niagara Falls (though the volume of water coming over Toccoa Falls is somewhat less). The fee to go to the base of the falls seems to have protected the area from the trashy littering usually found at many scenic view points

Toccoa Falls College, founded in 1907, is a four-year school affiliated with the Christian Missionary Alliance, and most of its 1,200 students go into church work.

A half-mile north of Toccoa Falls College, GA 17 Alt. enters the Chattahoochee National Forest. Covering more than 750,000 acres, this reserve of woodlands was created in 1936 when the North Georgia Mountains had been logged practically bare. Reclaimed by the Forest Service and Civilian Conservation Corps, it stretches across much of North Georgia. Many of

Toccoa Fall at Toccoa Falls College. The marker on the left memorializes the people who died during a flood on November 6, 1977, when 176 million gallons of water smashed through the campus.

the opportunities for outdoor activities in the region are on national forest land. It is not a solid mass of forest, and private landholdings mottle the national forest map.

You may notice that the highway here is straighter than average in this region, and is made of thick concrete. Local lore says it was paved after World War II as a political reward. The paving is in remarkably good shape, and has needed few repairs in the past half century.

About 8 miles from Toccoa Falls College, cross GA 365/US 441. This recently constructed four-lane road is an extension of I-985 near Gainesville, giving easy access to these northeast Georgia mountains. Across GA 365, you come to Hollywood. There are convenience stores here, plus a pottery store.

Turn left onto Old U.S. Highway 441 (US 441 Bus.). At 2 miles on the right sits the old summer home of Joseph Habersham, the man for whom this county was named. He was a Revolutionary War soldier, politician, and Postmaster General from 1795 to 1801 under Presidents Washington, Adams, and Jefferson.

Two and a half miles past the Habersham home, you enter Clarkesville. The town has converted its downtown from serving local farmers and housewives to supplying mountain-bound tourists. The town square is filled with shops offering antiques, crafts, gifts, and books, and cafes and restaurants, all in refurbished storefronts dating to the turn of the century. The local bank on the square serves double-duty as a welcome center and financial institution.

A few blocks from the square, US 441 Bus. passes the very attractive Presbyterian Church and the Charm House. This large house on the left has been a doctor's office, hospital, and restaurant, and is now a bed and breakfast inn.

Three miles from Clarkesville is the village of Demorest. It features several appealing shops in a small business district. On the left side of the road stands Piedmont College. Affiliated with the Congregational Christian Church, this small school has an enrollment of around 400 students. At the peak of the spire of the school chapel is a gold weathervane shaped like the Mayflower. For baseball buffs, Demorest was the home of Johnny "Big Cat" Mize.

Stay on US 441 Bus. for 4 miles to Cornelia. Pick up Georgia Highway 105 into downtown where The Big Red Apple is at the railroad depot. It is a 5,200-pound concrete representation saluting apple growers. Cornelia claims this is the largest apple monument in the world.

Continue to follow GA 105 out of Cornelia, across the Banks County line, and (still following GA 105) turn left onto the Ty Cobb Parkway. Nicknamed "The Georgia Peach," Ty Cobb was one of the fiercest competitors

*This 5,200 pound concrete apple is a tribute to the
apple growers of the Cornelia area.*

the game of baseball has ever seen. He was born in Banks County in 1886 and died in Royston in 1961 (see Drive 14). A historic marker at this turn tells of the Battle of Narrows, a skirmish at a nearby mountain pass in 1864. It was one of the few Civil War engagements in the northeast part of the state.

Stay on GA 105 for 9 miles, then turn left on Georgia Highway 184. You will cross the Stephens County line and in 4 miles come to Currahee Baptist Church. This area gives you an excellent view of Currahee Mountain. Unfortunately, the scenic beauty of this granite outcrop is marred by the various antennas and communication transmission towers built atop it. The unsightly towers may one day be replaced by less obtrusive equipment.

Currahee Mountain stays visible on your left as you continue to the GA 17 bypass around Toccoa. You can continue straight and return to Toccoa, or take GA 17 north to GA 365, or south back to Georgia Highways 106 and 320 to I-85.

14

Georgia Granite
Elberton to Hartwell to Royston

General description: The 35-mile drive begins at Elberton, the heart of granite quarrying, and continues past the Georgia Guidestones, 20-foot high granite monoliths, espousing the conservation of mankind. Paralleling the Savannah River, impounded by Russell and Hartwell lakes, Georgia Highway 77 goes to the town of Hartwell. From here it leads to Royston, home of baseball great Ty Cobb and Victoria Bryant State Park.

Special attractions: Granite quarries, artistic stonework, Georgia Guidestones, Hartwell, Royston's Cobb Memorial, Victoria Bryant State Park, and historic Elberton.

Location: Northeast Georgia just south of Interstate 85.

Drive route numbers: Georgia Highways 368, 77, 327, and 17; and U.S. Highway 29.

Travel season: All year.

Camping: Hart State Park and Victoria Bryant State Park.

Services: Motels, fine restaurants, and gasoline are located in all the larger towns. State park campgrounds have water, electricity hookups, and dump stations.

Nearby attractions: Russell Lake, Hartwell Lake, and their dams and powerhouses; trout fishing below the dams and warmwater fishing in the lakes is usually good. Hart State Park on Hartwell Lake; Hart County Wildlife Management Area offers deer, turkey and small game hunting in season; and Lake Richard B. Russell State Park.

The drive

This short drive through the northeast Georgia Piedmont region offers a number of interesting stops and side trips with something for a range of interests and tastes. First, there is Elberton, which calls itself "Granite Capitol of the World" with good reason. More tombstones, or monuments as they are euphemistically termed, are made here than anywhere else in the world. For over a hundred years, workers have cut stone from local quarries, and there is plenty more stone left. If you are intrigued by mystery, or philosophy, or the bizarre, you may enjoy another monument of sorts, called the Georgia Guidestones, an "American Stonehenge." Baseball fans will want

Sunrise from Brasstown Bald, Drive 10, Helen to Brasstown Bald

Top: *Etowah Indian Mounds, Drive 5, Land of the Cherokees*
Bottom: *Bavarian-style village of Helen, Drive 10, Helen to Brasstown Bald*

Waterfall in Tallulah Gorge, Drive 11, Clarksville to Tallulah Gorge

Top: *Saint Simons Lighthouse, Drive 29, Georgia Coast*
Bottom: *Sunset, shrimp boats, and Altamaha River, Drive 29, Georgia Coast*

Sunset at Banks Lake, Drive 27, Valdosta to Thomasville

Providence Canyon State Park, Drive 22, Columbus to Providence Canyon

Top: *Dahlonega Gold Museum, Drive 9, Gold Rush*
Bottom: *Vogel State Park, Drive 9, Gold Rush*

Toccoa Falls, Drive 13, Toccoa Loop

Drive 14: Georgia Granite

Elberton to Hartwell to Royston

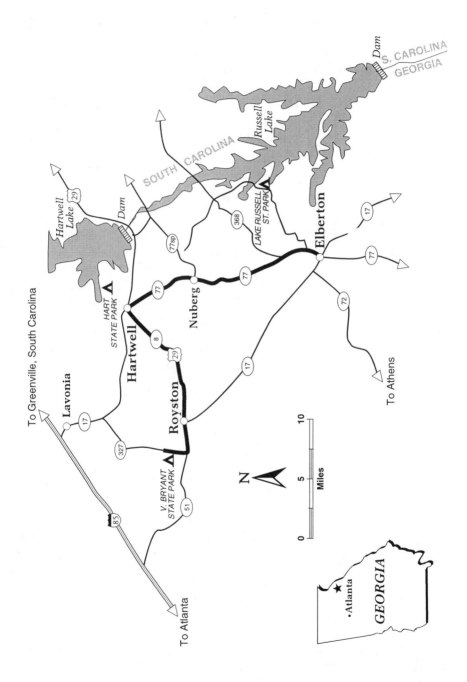

to visit Royston, the hometown and final resting place of Tyrus Raymond "Ty" Cobb, one of the finest and fiercest players the game has ever seen. For recreation and relaxation, the drive ends at Victoria Bryant State Park, where you can camp, hike, picnic, fish, swim, or play a round of golf.

The nearby waters of Hartwell Lake and Russell Lake, impoundments of the Savannah River, offer camping, boating, and fishing. Thirty-six miles to the southwest via Georgia Highway 72 is Athens, the home of the University of Georgia, which offers myriad pleasures. Thirty miles south of Elberton is Washington, whose antebellum homes and Revolutionary War battlefield are a terminus of Drive 16, Augusta to Washington. To the north of Royston is Toccoa, the subject of Drive 13, Toccoa Loop. Interstate highway access is from I-85 at any Georgia exit north of Commerce, which offers bargain shopping at outlet stores and flea markets.

The drive begins in Elberton at Granite Center, headquarters of the Elbert Granite Association, on GA 72, 0.5 mile west of GA 77. Here you can get directions to one of the more than forty active quarries in the area that cut the famous blue-gray Elberton granite. The Granite Museum is open each afternoon, displaying artifacts from a century of the stone business. Featured is "Dutchy," possibly the first statue made of Elberton Granite. Dutchy was carved in the 1880s, when an itinerant German stonecutter was commissioned by local folk who wanted a statue of a confederate soldier for the Elberton courthouse square. Unfortunately, the stonecutter carved a figure the Elberton population felt looked more like a "Pennsylvania Dutchman," wearing a Union uniform to boot. The statue was toppled and buried where it fell. In 1976, Dutchy was exhumed and moved to the museum.

Leaving Granite Center and turning left (east) on GA 72, you pass Elbert County High School and its athletic field, The Granite Bowl. Set in a valley, this 20,000-seat stadium is made, naturally, of granite. It is hard to exaggerate how important granite is to the town. There are granite signs, granite walls, and granite buildings. Stone companies and monument companies line all the highways into town.

Turn left onto GA 77. Notice the display of monuments on the corner. Granite comes in a number of hues, including blue, red, gray, and black. Elbert County granite is blue-gray. Stone of other colors from quarries around the world is brought here to be cut and polished by Elberton's skilled artisans.

Go by Veterans Memorial, a tribute to armed services in etched stone (need we say what kind?), past granite sheds of some of more than 150 companies where the granite is cut with giant wire saws, polished, and made into tombstones.

Seven miles north of town on GA 77 stands The Georgia Guidestones. Guidestones Road leads to the right to a parking area. This 19-foot-high

Granite quarry near Elberton, the largest granite-producing area in the world.

"American Stonehenge" offers guidelines for civilization in eight modern and four ancient languages. Its specifications were given and construction was paid for by a group whose identity has been kept secret.

Continuing north on GA 77, in a mile you cross Hart County line. Hart County and its seat, Hartwell, are named for Nancy Hart, a local woman who carried on a spirited private vendetta against the British and their sympathizers during the American Revolution. She was known as "War Woman" to the Cherokees. Her cabin was actually in Elbert County, 10 miles south of Elberton at Broad River.

Continue north along pastures interspersed with sections of pines and hardwoods, typical rolling Piedmont countryside. At Liberty Hill Church Road sits a genuine old-time country store. These used to be common, but now they are being replaced, even in rural areas, by modern "convenience stores."

Hartwell is a medium-sized town (pop. 5,000) with neat homes on either side of the road. Their styles, ranging from Victorian to ranch, indicate the general time each was built.

Turn right on U.S. Highway 29, getting to the left lane as you swing around to follow the road south toward Royston. Continuing following US 29, and turn left onto East Franklin Street. On the left is the Judy Theatre. Closed now, it is a Quonset hut style building, which dates it around World War II when these buildings were developed.

Georgia Guidestones, "American Stonehenge." Each pillar is inscribed in a different language, both modern and ancient.

Continue to follow US 29 as it winds its way out of town about 2 miles to a granite marker and historical sign marking the place Cherokees called *Ah-Yeh-Li A-Lo-Hee*, "The Center of the World," which was an assembly place for councils, trade, and worship. Considering the Georgia Guidestones are not far from here, maybe the Cherokees and builders of the Guidestones had similar feelings.

Farther on past Goldmine community, you can see vestiges of the path where this highway previously ran. They veer to the side, crossing streams on old bridges now overgrown with trees and vines. The current US 29 obviously straightened these old curves.

Royston is best known as home of Ty Cobb, considered by many to be one of the finest baseball players in history. Although many thought Cobb had at best an abrasive personality, he made civic contributions to Royston, funding construction of Cobb Memorial Hospital on US 29 on the east side of town. At the Civic Center and City Hall across the street from the hospital is a bust of Cobb, engraved with some of the statistics of his baseball career from 1904–1928. There is a library next door with a number of reference works on Cobb and his life and exploits. After his death in 1961, his body was placed in a mausoleum at Rosehill Cemetery. To reach the cemetery, turn left at the traffic light in the center of town and go south on GA 17 for 0.7 mile to the cemetery gate on the left. The Cobb mausoleum is straight ahead.

Two miles on US 29 east of Royston is Franklin Springs, home of Emmanuel College, affiliated with the Pentecostal Holiness Church, on the left. A mile and a half past the college, turn right onto Georgia Highway 327 toward Victoria Bryant State Park. Notice the house on the left, with yard ornaments including a dummy bomb labeled, "Big Bullet."

A mile farther, turn left into Victoria Bryant State Park. This 406-acre facility offers tent and RV camping, swimming pool, picnic shelters, fishing lake, 5 miles of hiking trails, and a nine-hole golf course.

Drive 15: Covington to Crawfordville

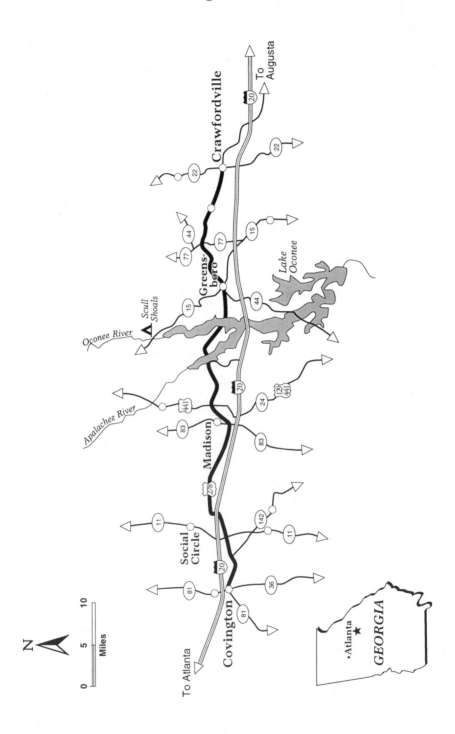

15

Covington to Crawfordville

General description: For 60 miles, this drive follows U.S. Highway 278 from Covington to Crawfordville. Interstate 20 now carries the heavy traffic between Atlanta and Augusta, making the older U.S. highway is less busy, so you can enjoy the rural countryside and small, historical towns.

Special attractions: Restored antebellum homes in Madison; cultural and historic museums; Lake Oconee and Oconee National Forest; two state parks; recreation areas on Lake Oconee; excellent golf courses; hunting and fishing in the national forest and on Lake Oconee; and background locations for several movies and television series.

Location: East of Atlanta in the heart of the Piedmont. US 278 parallels and is mostly north of I-20 between Atlanta and Augusta.

Drive route number: U.S. Highway 278

Travel season: A year-round drive. The hardwood forests along the way are colorful beginning in late September and continuing, in some years, into late October. In spring, dogwoods, redbuds, red maples, yellow jasmine, and other flowering trees and shrubs make a colorful show.

Camping: Tent and trailer camp sites are available at Hard Labor Creek State Park and A. H. Stephens State Historic Park. Georgia Power Company recreation sites on Lake Oconee have campsites and commercial campgrounds are near Madison and Crawfordville. Primitive camping is permitted in some areas of the Oconee National Forest.

Services: Motels, bed and breakfasts, gas stations, and restaurants are located in Covington, Madison, and Greensboro. Billie's Blue Willow Inn in Social Circle, north of US 278 on GA 11, is a well-known eating spot.

Nearby attractions: Watson Mill Bridge State Park; Mistletoe State Park; Fox Vineyards Winery near Covington; 1996 Summer Olympic Equestrian venue at Georgia International Horse Park near Conyers.

 The drive

This drive goes from Covington east to Crawfordville on US 278. This federal highway parallels I-20, traveling east and west. Since I-20 was completed in the late 1960s, traffic on US 278 in rural areas has become generally light and local. The road goes through the Piedmont, following an ancient Creek Indian trading route that became an avenue for emigrants settling the Southeast in the early nineteenth century. The countryside rolls gently through pastures, through sections of the Oconee National Forest, and through a number of small towns established before the Civil War. The Georgia Railroad from Atlanta to Augusta was built here in the 1830s. It was this rail line that Union General William Tecumseh Sherman followed, ripping up the tracks and destroying the roadbed, on his famous "March to the Sea." Madison was spared the torch of Sherman's troops, and calls itself "The Town Sherman Refused to Burn." Many of its antebellum houses have been maintained or restored to their original beauty, and their current residents open them for tours several times a year. The drive ends outside Crawfordville at Liberty Hill, the home of Alexander Stephens, vice-president of the Confederacy. In recent years, Hollywood has found this area. Movie production companies discovered towns like Covington, Madison, and Crawfordville and have used them as backgrounds for a number of feature films as well as at least three television series.

Crawfordville and Greensboro are stops on one of the Classic South driving tours of the East Central Georgia Travel Association, and Madison is located on Georgia's Antebellum Trail. Both Covington and Madison are on the Georgia Antiques Trail.

This drive is near two other drives: Drives 16 and 17.

The drive begins in Covington at the intersection of I-20 and US 278. Heading east, shopping centers, fast-food outlets, and gas stations line this four-lane, undivided, busy thoroughfare. Emory Street leads left 2 miles to Oxford, Home of Oxford College, the original site of Emory University. There is a self-guided tour available (at the fudge shop) for this town, which, among other charms, has a tree that owns the land on which it grows.

Back on US 278 in Covington, a right onto Pace Street leads to the town square. A driving tour of Covington is available from the Covington/ Newton County Chamber of Commerce at 2100 Washington Street. It features the Floyd Street District of the National Register of Historic Places, with a number of antebellum and Victorian homes and churches. You may notice something familiar about the square, the Victorian Newton County courthouse on its north side, and the stores in the area, because this town was used as a site for the television series, *Dukes of Hazard*, and more recently, *In the Heat of the Night*. Television fans will recognize several of the locales used in these shows.

Back on US 278, continue east out of town, across the Alcovy River, and what has been called one of the purest examples of a tupelo gum river swamp still in existence. Near the intersection with GA 11, 7 miles from Covington, is a brick building on the left. The "Brick Store," built in 1822 at Newton County's first settlement, has been a courthouse, jail, school, and stagecoach inn as well as a store. You continue through pine and oak woods, along broad pastures, and cross Interstate 20. In 1.5 miles, the Walton State

Fish Hatchery is on the left, and on the right, the headquarters of the Wildlife Resources Division of the Georgia Department of Natural Resources.

Two miles later, you come to Rutledge. The town of Rutledge is to the left, across the railroad tracks. It has been renovated, and several of the old brick-front buildings now house antique and gift stores and restaurants. If you continue north through Rutledge, you will reach Hard Labor Creek State Park. This park, built by members of the Civilian Conservation Corps during the depression of the 1930s, has camping facilities, picnic grounds, hiking trails, a lake for fishing and swimming, and an eighteen-hole golf course.

Continuing on US 278, 7 miles from Rutledge, you enter the city of Madison. Established in 1809, Madison was an important stop along the stagecoach road from Charleston to New Orleans decades before Atlanta was even dreamed of. Many of its homes date to the early part of the nineteenth century, and are proudly shown by their owners during several tours of homes held each year. The brick building on the right, now called the Madison-Morgan Cultural Center, is the former Madison Elementary School. This Romanesque Revival building built in 1895 is now home to art exhibits, professional theatrical productions, and a museum. As a nod to its origins, several of the old schoolrooms are preserved much as they were when educating children was the business of the place.

Morgan County African American Museum on Academy Street is located in a 1895 farm home, and spotlights the contributions African-Americans have made to the culture of the South.

Entering the center of the town, you will find a number of eating establishments on and near the square. The Chamber of Commerce, on the northeast side of the square, can provide information on walking tours, tours of homes, and on the several bed and breakfasts operating in Madison.

About 5 miles from Madison, Buckhead Road bears right leading 2 miles to Buckhead, Georgia. It is not to be confused with the section of Atlanta called "Buckhead." The people of the Morgan County Buckhead (population 300) pride themselves on being the only true Buckhead, a real town with a zip code (30625).

Four miles past Buckhead Road, US 278 crosses the Apalachee River which, at this point, is part of Lake Oconee, an impoundment formed by the Apalachee and Oconee Rivers. Five and a half miles later, you cross the Oconee River arm of Lake Oconee. In the distance to the left, you can see a small island in the lake. This is Dyer Mound, constructed during the Mississippian Period between A.D. 500 and 1500, and was flooded as the water rose in the young impoundment. Archaeologists have determined that it is a "midden mound," or, to be more blunt, an aboriginal trash dump. On the right, on the far side of the river bridge, is the entrance to the Redlands

Recreation Area. It is administered by the USDA Forest Service, and is part of Oconee National Forest. It serves mainly as a boat launch area for Lake Oconee.

In about 4 miles, you enter Greensboro. It was founded in 1786 and was burned a year later by the Creek Indians. The town "gaol" built in 1807 is patterned after European bastilles. It squats on Green Street behind the courthouse, looking much like a small castle keep. The walls are solid stone, and inside on the second floor, the trap door of the gallows is still operable.

For a side trip, travel approximately 14 miles from Greensboro north on Georgia Highway 15, across the Oconee River. In the middle of a field, you will see the Iron Horse, a 2,000-pound statue originally placed in front of a dormitory at the University of Georgia. Its appearance inspired such vandalism and desecration that the statue was removed and stored until L. C. Curtis acquired it and gave it its present home in this field. Also in this area are the ruins of Scull Shoals, a manufacturing town circa 1812. It is on the Greensboro side of the river, and is reached by a short hike from Oconee River Recreation Area or by following Macedonia Road and Forest Road 1234.

Continuing west from Greensboro on US 278, you parallel the Georgia Railroad, which was dismantled by Sherman's Union troops. Bonfires were built of the crossties, and the rails were laid across the fire to heat in order to be wrapped around trees. The resulting "Sherman's neckties" were worthless for further use.

Seven miles from Greensboro is Union Point, home of the Chipman Union hosiery factory, which is on the National Register of Historic Places. A factory store behind the factory (on your left as you go through town) sells socks and other items to bargain hunters.

As you continue the 12 miles to Crawfordville, you are traveling a portion of the English–Indian Common Road leading from Charleston, South Carolina, to Vicksburg, Mississippi. It was in use by white explorers as early as 1698. English merchants used the route to trade with the Indian nations, and after Georgia was established in 1732, it was traveled by such notables as naturalist William Bartram and Revolutionary war hero, the Marquis de LaFayette. You may have seen Crawfordville's downtown in any of a half dozen feature films shot here including *Paris Trout* and *Home Fires Burning*. Turn left at the Talliaferro (pronounced "TAHL-uh-ver") County Courthouse to go to Liberty Hill, home of Alexander Stephens, vice-president of the Confederacy. It is maintained and operated by the state of Georgia, and offers tours of the home and surrounding buildings. Continuing past Liberty Hill, you will come to Alexander Stephens State Park, which offers picnicking, camping, and other outdoor recreation.

16

Augusta to Washington
Up Washington Road

General description: Beginning at the Fall Line near Augusta, this drive traverses the Piedmont region and its small farms and forested areas. The area is steeped in history, from the Augusta Canal to the Robert Toombs House and the Washington Presbyterian Church organized in 1790. The drive crosses one arm of Clarks Hill Lake (known in South Carolina as J. Strom Thurmond Lake), and a number of side trips can be made to the U. S. Army Corps of Engineers recreation areas and other points of interest on the lake.

Special attractions: Augusta is the site of the Medical College of Georgia; the Masters Golf Tournament; the 1886 Cotton Exchange; many historic homes; and the River Walk with many special events, especially boat races and other water sports. Mistletoe State Park on Clarks Hill Lake has hiking trails and a swimming beach. Clarks Hill Dam area has attractive picnicking areas and fishing pier in the river below the dam.

Location: Eastern border of Georgia, north and northwest of Augusta.

Drive route numbers: Interstate 20, Georgia Highways 104 and 47, county roads to Augusta Canal and Dam, and U.S. Highways 378 and 78.

Travel season: Year-round, with highlights in spring for flowering shrubs and trees, and fall for leaf color. The lakes offer year-round fishing.

Camping: U.S. Army Corps of Engineers recreation sites; Mistletoe and Elijah Clark state parks all have tent, trailer, and RV camping.

Services: Many fine restaurants and lodging in the Augusta area, Lincolnton, and Washington.

Nearby attractions: Clarks Hill Lake and Dam; Fort Gordon Military Reservation; Mistletoe and Elijah Clark state parks.

 The drive

The drive begins by paralleling the Savannah River north of Augusta, which is the state line between South Carolina and Georgia, connecting two of Georgia's older cities via a route that dates to the eighteenth century. Augusta and Washington both have rich histories. Augusta, named for the Mother of England's King George III, began as a fort in 1735, and was an important trading post and departure point for settlers heading west. Wash-

Drive 16: Augusta to Washington
Up Washington Road

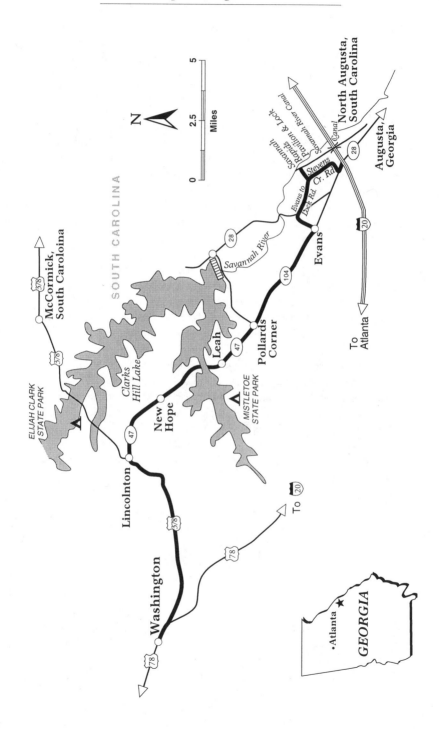

ington, the first city named for George Washington, dates to land treaties with the Creeks and Cherokees in 1773. Near Washington, the Battle of Kettle Creek in 1779 halted British incursion into northeastern Georgia. Augusta, site of many military engagements, was captured twice by the British during the American Revolution. During the Civil War, Augusta was an important manufacturer of armaments and gunpowder, and Washington was home to Confederate Secretary of State Robert Toombs. Both towns have a wealth of homes and buildings dating to their early days.

Augusta is now best known as home of the Masters Golf Tournament, played at Augusta National Golf Club each April. Augusta National is on Washington Road, 1.2 miles south of I-20. Unfortunately, this golfing shrine is open to the public only for the week of the tournament, and tickets for the event are routinely sold out. The good news is, Augusta and Washington are full of interesting things much more accessible than Augusta National.

Washington Road (Georgia Highways 104 and 47) is the main route between the two towns. It runs parallel to the Savannah River, touches Clarks Hill Lake (known as J. Strom Thurmond Lake in South Carolina), passes through Lincolnton, and ends in Washington. It rolls over the gentle hills of the Piedmont the entire way.

The drive begins in Augusta on Washington Road at I-20. Go north on Washington Road under the Interstate, and turn right on Stevens Creek Road.

NOTE: In about 0.5 mile, Stevens Creek Road turns left. Be sure to follow Stevens Creek Road.

In about 3 miles, turn right onto Locks Road in Evans. A mile later, you reach the Savannah Rapids Pavilion of Columbia County. This meeting facility overlooks Augusta City Locks and Dam. Begun in 1845, the 9-mile-long Augusta Canal admitted boats loaded with cotton from upstream plantations to reach downtown Augusta. This allowed them to bypass shoals on the Savannah River, and helped make Augusta one of the world's largest inland cotton markets of the nineteenth century. It also provided water power for mills and drinking water for the city. It still fulfills the two latter functions, and as it has throughout its long history, also gives Augustans and visitors an area for recreation and relaxation.

Large oaks shading the riverbank wear gray beards of Spanish moss. Augusta is near the northernmost edge of the range of this bromeliad that lives on airborne nutrients.

A walking and bicycling trail follows the levee between the canal and the river, and canoeists and fishers find adventure in the canal and in the river.

Augusta is at the head of navigation of the Savannah River, sitting on

Augusta Locks, Dam, and Canal at Savannah Rapids Pavilion.

the Fall Line, the geographical break between the Coastal Plain and the Piedmont, which runs across the state from Augusta to Columbus. Shoals that made upstream travel impossible at the Fall Line also provided ready power for mills and made the Fall Line cities of Augusta, Macon, and Columbus important industrial centers.

Head back out of Evans to Locks Road for 6 miles, then turn right onto Washington Road (GA 104). The rest of this trip, some 50 miles, will be on Washington Rd.

In about 3.5 miles there is a notable display of lawn ornaments decorating the home on the left. The residents here have surpassed mere acreage accessorization and have made their house a showplace of outdoor statuary.

Georgia Highways 104, 150, 57, and 47, and US Highway 221 intersect at Pollards Corner—a very small crossroads to be carrying so many numbers. GA 104 ends at this intersection.

Pick up GA 47 and continue straight. A sign at the corner indicates Mistletoe State Park is 10 miles to the left, on GA 150.

As you travel upcountry from the Fall Line, the dirt changes from the sandy soil of the Coastal Plain to the famous Georgia red clay of the Piedmont. Agriculture in this area consists mostly of livestock raising, with pastures and forests making up most of the land.

The famed naturalist and botanist William Bartram followed this route through Georgia in 1765 and 1773, collecting botanical specimens. His diaries describe the people and places he visited on his trips; his route is memorialized by the Bartram Trail. Of "the village of Augusta," he pronounced, "The site . . . is perhaps the most delightful and eligible of any in Georgia for a city."

At Keg Creek, the road crosses a small arm of Clarks Hill Lake. Ridge Park, a Corps of Engineers recreation area, is to the right. Clarks Hill Lake, covering 70,000 acres and with over 1,200 miles of shoreline, is the largest Corps of Engineers project east of the Mississippi. It offers swimming, camping, picnicking, fishing, and some of the finest publicly owned hunting lands in the state.

Robert Toombs Home Museum and Historic Site in Washington.

Fourteen miles north of the bridge over the Little River branch of Clarks Hill Lake, you enter Lincolnton, the seat of Lincoln County. Both are named for General Benjamin Lincoln, who served in the American Revolution, and not for President Abraham Lincoln. We would not want you to think the folks in this area suffered a fit of remorse for seceding from the Union and decided to honor "Honest Abe." Elijah Clark State Park is to the east of Lincolnton off Georgia 43 and U.S. Highway 378. The Lincolnton–Lincoln County Chamber of Commerce offers guides and tours of the area's many attractions, including over 200 homes and buildings on the National Register.

Stay on GA 47 as it turns left, joining US 278 West toward Washington. This pleasant drive through mixed hardwood and pine forests and through open pastures where cattle graze bears few scars to remind you that this land was farmed practically to death in the days when cotton was the main crop. After the soil was depleted, most of the farming died out and many residents moved away. Those who remained turned to cattle production or let their land lie fallow. This is one reason for all the timber and pasture in the area.

Just outside Washington, pick up US 78, continuing on GA 47 straight into Washington. Washington has two national landmarks, and two districts and fourteen individual sites on the National Register of Historic Places. Before you reach the center of town, you will pass the Washington–Wilkes Historical Museum. This antebellum home displays many Indian and Civil War artifacts, including the field desk of Confederate President Jefferson Davis, who held the last meeting with his cabinet in Washington, Georgia, not D.C., as they all fled Union troops in 1865. Continue into town past the home of Robert Toombs, Secretary of State of the confederacy. His home is now a state-operated museum.

You can backtrack and return to Augusta or, if you prefer, you may reach Interstate 20 via Georgia Highways 44, 47, and 80, or US 78.

17

Covington to Milledgeville Loop

Eatonton, Monticello, Panola Mountain

General description: On this drive, you travel between two important watersheds in Georgia, the Oconee River and the Ocmulgee River—typical Piedmont country with its scattered farmland and forests. The drive crosses portions of the Oconee National Forest, ending at Panola Mountain Conservation Park, a large granite dome only about 20 miles from downtown Atlanta.

Special attractions: Peaceful, rural countryside; Uncle Remus Museum and Park; Rock Eagle 4-H Center; historic Milledgeville, the former capital of Georgia; historic homes predating the Civil War; Baldwin Forest Public Fishing Area; Lockerly Arboretum; and Panola Mountain Conservation Park.

Location: The heartland of Georgia, almost in the center of the state.

Drive route numbers: U.S. Highways 278 and 441; Georgia Highways 142, 16, 22, 212 and 138.

Travel season: All year. Spring is best for flowering shrubs and trees in the formal gardens. The great variety of deciduous and evergreen trees creates impressive fall colors, only without the heavy traffic of the mountain drives.

Camping: Lake Sinclair Recreation Area in Oconee National Forest has excellent camping facilities from late May to Labor Day.

Services: Fine hotels, motels, and bed and breakfasts are available in all the larger towns, especially Covington, Eatonton, and Milledgeville. Fine restaurants are also found all along the drive.

Nearby attractions: Boating at Lake Oconee and Jackson Lake; also, Piedmont National Wildlife Refuge and Lake Sinclair Recreation Area.

 The drive

This 150-mile loop covers a lot of area and a multitude of attractions. There is enough variety on this trip to arouse a spectrum of interests—from Covington, with its antebellum homes to Eatonton's Rock Eagle effigy mound and tales of Uncle Remus to Milledgeville, the capital of the state during the Civil War, to Monticello's movie locations to the Monastery of the Holy Spirit and Panola Mountain's natural wonders. It would be wise to allow a couple days for the complete trip, with a stopover in Milledgeville to tour the many features of that city.

Drive 17: Covington to Milledgeville Loop

Eatonton, Monticello, Panola Mountain

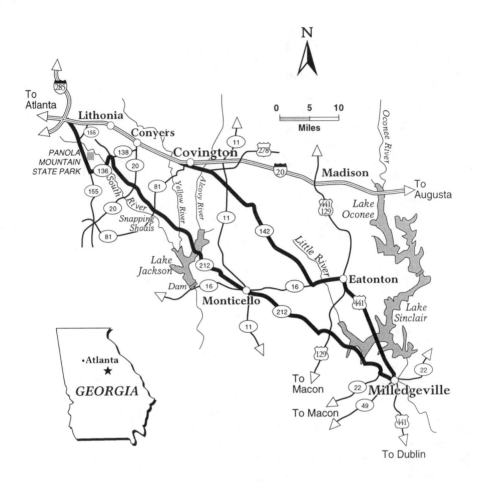

Covington, the starting point of the drive, is also the beginning of Drive 15, Covington to Crawfordville. Other drives close by are Drive 18, Piedmont Loop; and Drive 19, Kaolin Loop.

Two river systems bound the trip. To the east, the Oconee is dammed twice, forming Lake Oconee to the north near Eatonton, and below that, Lake Sinclair near Milledgeville. On the west, the South River, Yellow River, and Alcovy River join at Jackson Lake near Monticello, forming the Ocmulgee River. The Oconee and Ocmulgee eventually unite near Lumber City forming the Altamaha, which flows into the Atlantic Ocean near Darien.

Dairy farming is a major activity in this part of Georgia's Piedmont.

According to figures for 1989, there were more than 54,000 cattle in the counties covered by this trip, with 21,000 in Putnam County alone. In Putnam, there are approximately 2 cows for every human resident. As recently as the 1950s, this was an area of small family farms futilely trying to produce a profit on land worn out by cotton farming. Many residents left the agricultural life to work in textile mills or in the cities of Atlanta and Macon. Their land lay fallow and grew trees and pasture grass, and now there are only occasional glimpses of the past in abandoned farm homes and barns, in sentinel chimneys of burned houses, and in gullies eroded in fields now grown over with pine, oak, and yellow poplar. Newton and Rockdale counties in particular are becoming bedroom communities for Atlanta, and residential developments are growing on land that once made cotton king.

Before Europeans came to America, this land was populated by nomad hunters as much as 10,000 years ago. They were followed by the mound builders of the Mississippian culture, who raised corn and worshiped the sun from atop earthen mounds and built giant effigies of animals, such as the Rock Eagle near Eatonton. This culture was nearly dead by the time European exploration started in the sixteenth century. The mound builders were replaced by the Creeks, who were a fiercely territorial farming society, and conducted frequent feuds over land. Then came white settlers, and by 1827, the Creeks had ceded all the land in this area to the United States, although bands of Creeks continued raids in Georgia until 1838.

During the Civil War, the region grew crops to feed the Confederate Army. After the fall of Atlanta in 1864, General Sherman's Union armies converged through this area as they made their way to the state capitol in Milledgeville. From there, they forged east to Savannah in the famous "March to the Sea."

Milledgeville and Eatonton are part of Georgia's Antebellum Trail, and Covington, Eatonton, and Milledgeville are on the Antiques Trail. Interstate 20 provides access to this drive at Covington.

The drive begins on US 278 at Georgia Highway 36 (Pace Street) in Covington. Covington's town square is on GA 36 south of US 278 and may look familiar. It has been used as background in a number of movies and in *The Dukes of Hazard* and *Heat of the Night* television series (see Drive 15). The local visitor center on Elm Street can provide self-guided walking and driving tours of the town's many historic sites.

Travel east on US 278, and at the edge of town you pick up GA 142, continuing east. A mile later you cross the Alcovy River, where the Georgia Wildlife Federation is building a nature center in this rare example of a Piedmont gum swamp.

A mile past the river, bear right, following GA 142 and leaving US 278. You cross Georgia Highway 11, and soon the road is flanked by two older homes with attractive stonework walls and nice trees and shrubbery. This area is marked by small streams and swampy bottomlands.

Newborn, the next community you reach, was an active trading center years ago where farmers brought their cotton to be ginned and bought their provisions at the local stores. Now it is a sleepy village with a few open stores and empty shells of others. Down the road is the community of Broughton, where there are store buildings and an old ginhouse from the days when this area was farmed extensively for cotton. Fifty years ago, small cotton farms covered this area. The land became depleted, and many farms were abandoned. Weather eroded the worn-out soil and formed deep gullies over the barren hills. The land has regenerated, but you can still see areas where gullies were washed out. It is interesting to note that almost all the trees here are less than fifty years old, yet the area is heavily forested.

Past Broughton is a pecan grove, one of the crops farmers turned to when the cotton economy collapsed. The pecan grove is followed by a thick stand of pine trees, which have become a major crop on this land. It takes twenty years or more for this crop to be ready for harvesting for pulpwood or lumber, but it is a crop like any other.

Three miles past Broughton at the intersection with GA 83 is Shadydale, a pleasant residential community of turn-of-the-century homes. Little is left of the downtown area except an old bank building, an old store building, and the old town well, which is marked as being a former stagecoach stop.

Georgia's Civil War era capitol is now the administration building for Georgia Military Academy in Milledgeville.

Continuing on GA 142, you enter Putnam County, which calls itself the Dairy Capital of Georgia. You will see a number of large pastures with cows grazing all along this route. In some areas, gullies left from the days when erosion became a problem are a reminder of the past. A relic of the struggle to control erosion is kudzu. This quick-growing plant was introduced to America from Japan, and during the 1930s was widely planted to help control erosion. It was a successful solution, but kudzu itself became a problem because, if not controlled, it will take over fields, trees, houses, or anything else that stands still long enough.

Should you take this drive in the winter, you will see many small dirt mounds, evidence of another foreign invader. These are fire ant mounds. The fire ant is a South American insect that hitchhiked to the United States in the 1950s aboard freighters that landed at Mobile, Alabama. Despite extensive eradication programs, it has spread through much of the South from Virginia to Texas. It gets its name from its fiery bite.

GA 142 ends when you reach GA 16. Turn left, going east toward Eatonton. In case you have not yet seen any, a stand of kudzu is just across the Little River.

Just west of Eatonton, GA 16 meets US 441. About 5 miles north of Eatonton on this federal highway, at Rock Eagle 4-H Club Center, is a stone effigy mound shaped like a bird. It was constructed by prehistoric Indians who piled milky quartz rocks as much as 10 feet high to create the figure with a wingspan of 102 feet. It can be viewed from a tower built by the Civilian Conservation Corps in 1937. The 4-H Club Center also has picnic areas, boating, and a 110-acre fishing lake open to the public.

Eatonton is best known as the birthplace of writer Joel Chandler Harris, creator of Uncle Remus, whose tales of B'rer Rabbit, B'rer Fox, and B'rer Bear are retellings of African folk fables. GA 16 and US 441 Bus. reach the courthouse square in the center of town. In the road median as you enter the courthouse square is the usual Confederate monument. But most unusual is the statue on the east side of the square of B'rer Rabbit, the hero of most of the Uncle Remus tales. South of the square, on US 441 Bus., is the Uncle Remus Museum. Housed in a small building constructed from parts of three slave cabins, it is operated by the people of Eatonton.

Past the museum, on the left, is the Horton Homes factory. This is one of America's largest makers of manufactured housing (also known as mobile homes, house trailers, modular homes, etc.).

About a mile after you rejoin US 441 is the track of a tornado that struck in October 1993. You can easily see the swath of destruction that felled trees and demolished homes and buildings.

About 2 miles later, smokestacks in the distance mark Plant Harley Branch, a steam-generating facility of Georgia Power Company on Lake Sinclair. Soon you start to encounter arms of the 15,000-acre lake. This, like all other lakes and ponds in this part of Georgia, is a manmade impound-ment. The steam plant, fired by coal, discharges warm water into the lake; the warm water attracts fish, which attract fishers. You will almost always see anglers in action in the often misty waters beside the plant.

Continue straight ahead, picking up US 441 Bus. into downtown Milledgeville. You will pass Penitentiary Square, so named because it was the site of the Georgia State Penitentiary from 1817 to 1868. It is now the site of Georgia College. As to how apt the location is, you will have to in-quire of the students. Past the college, turn left on Georgia Highway 49, West Hancock Street. On the right as you turn is the office of the president of Georgia College. It was once the governor's mansion when Milledgeville was the capital city of Georgia from 1803 to 1864. At the end of the block, in the old post office building on the right, is the Tourist and Convention Bu-reau. Here you can get information or take a two-hour trolley tour of the city.

Built specifically as the state capitol, Milledgeville has numerous his-toric buildings and sites, including the reconstructed capitol building, which is now the administration building of Georgia Military Academy. Just south of town on Georgia Highway 112 is Central State Hospital, Georgia's oldest and largest mental health facility. Visitors are welcome to tour a small mu-seum and to stroll around the grounds.

Also on the south end of Milledgeville, on US 441 Bus. (Irwinton Road), is Lockerly Arboretum, a 45-acre research and educational preserve, featur-ing trees and plants from around the world.

Backtracking north of town, turn left on US 441 where it turns to bypass Milledgeville. At the intersection with Georgia Highway 22, turn right onto GA 22. In about 0.5 mile, turn right onto GA 212. Twelve miles further, after you cross another arm of Lake Sinclair at Potato Creek, Twin Bridges Road (on the right) leads to Twin Bridges Recreation area on Lake Sinclair, which features camping, hiking trails, fishing, and other recreational facilities.

Continuing north on GA 212, just past the intersection with U.S. High-way 129, you will soon see a baseball field built by local people; this rustic facility is the setting for games many summer weekends. Shortly past the baseball field is the sign for Cedar Creek Wildlife Management Area (WMA). Some of the finest deer, turkey, and small game hunting opportunities in the state are in the area of this drive. The Georgia Department of Natural Re-sources maintains the WMA for public hunting and other outdoor activi-ties. The WMA, like most of this section of the drive, is within Oconee National Forest. This is why you do not see a lot of buildings or other devel-opment, but you do see a whole lot of woods.

*The Uncle Remus Museum with displays and history of Joel Chandler
Harris's stories about B'rer Rabbit and kin.*

Some 12 miles beyond the WMA, you once again cross the path of the October 1993 tornadoes. As you drive along here, you can often see the traces of the old roadbed where the highway once meandered and is now straightened to accommodate modern traffic.

As you enter Monticello on GA 212, all the houses seem to have been built in the early part of the twentieth century, but Forsyth Street (Georgia Highway 83 South) is a neighborhood of Victorian and antebellum homes. If the Jasper County Courthouse and Courthouse Square in Monticello look familiar, they were the background for the film, *My Cousin Vinnie.*

GA 212 goes around the square and turns right. If you do not turn right but go straight ahead, district ranger headquarters for Oconee National Forest are a half-block off the square. Here you can get information about facilities within the 11,500-acre forest. About 9 miles north of town on GA 212, you come to a four-way stop at Jackson Lake Road. You can reach Lloyd Shoals Dam, which impounds Jackson Lake, by turning left on this road. At the base of the dam is the origin of the Ocmulgee River. A mile north of Jackson Lake Road, GA 212 crosses the Alcovy River arm of Jackson Lake. Much of this portion of the drive is in the watershed of Jackson Lake, formed by the Alcovy, Yellow, and South rivers. Cross GA 36, the Yellow River, and GA 162. This state highway goes right to the old mill village of Porterdale. Of the three textile mills built on shoals of the Yellow River, only the Bibb Mill still operates.

GA 212 passes the South River near Snapping Shoals. There was once a mill here, too, and there is still some activity in the community. An iron bridge washed away in the floods of July 1994, and its wreckage is still visible in the river.

Continue on GA 212, crossing GA 81 and then GA 20. Be careful to note that GA 212 turns left just past the Georgia 20 intersection. About 4 miles later, you come to the entrance of the Monastery of the Holy Spirit, a Trappist monastery started here in the 1940s and built by the monks themselves. In addition to the monks' quarters and farm buildings is a chapel, a retreat house, and a store featuring religious items as well as bread baked by the monks and a greenhouse selling herbs, flowers, and bonsai grown on the premises.

Seven miles past the monastery, turn left on GA 138. On your right is Smyrna Campground, which still hosts annual camp meetings. It was once common for people in the South to gather at spots like this in the summer after their crops were laid by, and enjoy a week or two of church services and social gatherings. Originally staying in tents or in the open, many families eventually built cabins at the campground. The campground is open only for camp meetings.

After you cross the South River, turn right on Georgia Highway 155. Three miles later is the entrance to Panola Mountain Conservation Park, a well-preserved ecosystem on a large granite outcropping. There are many such outcroppings in this area, including the world's largest, Stone Mountain; most of the others however, have been damaged by quarrying and human use. This one remains largely pristine and is administrated by the State of Georgia as a teaching facility. The park offers nature trails and picnicking, but no camping. From late August into October these granite domes are covered with patches of yellow flowers locally called "Confederate daisies."

From here, you can follow GA 155 to Interstate 285, the perimeter highway around Atlanta.

18

Piedmont Loop

High Falls, Indian Springs, Juliette

General description: This is an 85-mile drive in the lower Piedmont and Fall Line regions. The roads lead through mixed hardwood and pine forests with timber harvest, farmland, and pasture. Three state parks, a national wildlife refuge, and a national forest add considerable interest to this drive through a land steeped in history.

Special attractions: High Falls, Indian Springs, and Jarrell Plantation state parks; Piedmont National Wildlife Refuge; Juliette, Georgia, with its Whistle Stop Cafe, the location for filming of *Fried Green Tomatoes*; fall leaf color and spring flowering plants.

Location: Lower Piedmont, about three-quarters of the way from Atlanta to Macon.

Drive route numbers: Interstate 75; High Falls Road; Georgia Highways 36, 42, 83, 11, and 16; U.S. Highway 23; Stokes Store Road; Blue Ridge School Road; and Juliette Road.

Travel season: Year-round, with spring (early April) and fall (late October) offering the most attractive flowers and leaf color.

Camping: Tent and RV camping at High Falls and Indian Springs state parks. Primitive camping in Oconee National Forest.

Services: Excellent food at the Whistle Stop Cafe in Juliette, or Fresh Air Barbecue near Jackson. Motels and service stations in most of the small towns along the drive. Rental cottages at Indian Springs State Park.

Nearby attractions: Oconee National Forest, Dauset Trails Nature Center, Lake Juliette, Cedar Creek Wildlife Management Area, Macon Cherry Blossom Festival in March, and Ocmulgee National Monument.

 The drive

This drive is a good alternative to going to the mountains for fall colors and blooming spring dogwood and azaleas. The route visits three of the state parks in Georgia's lower Piedmont.

At Exit 65 from I-75, go east on High Falls Road for about 1 mile to the entrance to High Falls State Park. You might use this park as the starting point for the drive by camping at the park, taking in all the grandeur of the old dam, lake, falls below the dam, hiking trails, and fishing in the lake. The historical significance of this area is to be found in the hydro-power generated from Towaliga River and the use made of it in the manufacturing industry that supported a sizable town during pre- and post-Civil War times.

Leave the park and continue on High Falls Rd. to the intersection of GA 36. High Falls Rd. is two-lane and paved for about 6 miles, passing through rolling farmland with Christmas tree farms, cattle, pine plantations, and mixed pine-hardwood forests. Turn right, still traveling on GA 36, and in about 3 miles you are in Jackson. Here you pick up US 23; in the center of town, you pass the beautiful old red brick Butts County Courthouse, which is historic landmark. Northwest of town is one of Georgia's state prisons. The Jackson Diagnostic and Classification Center houses Georgia's Death Row, and is where the state administers the death penalty with the electric chair.

Continue through Jackson on US 23/GA 42 south for 5 miles. On the way, you pass the famous Fresh Air Barbecue restaurant, which has been in continuous operation since 1926. At the fork where GA 42 turns to the right, leaving US 23, there is an Indian Springs State Park sign. Go about a mile on GA 42 to the park entrance. Indian Springs is the site of historic Indian treaties and was once an elaborate spa with several fine hotels. This is considered to be one of the oldest state parks in the United States.

The sulfur-water springs were attractive to American Indians and white settlers alike. Today people still come to the springs to collect the mineral-rich water for drinking and medicinal uses. The old stone buildings and walkways are examples of how important the springs were to earlier cultures. A museum displays some of the Creek Indian, the early resort, and Civilian Conservation Corps history. Excellent hiking, picnicking, camping, swimming, boating, and cottage facilities are available here. Across GA 42 is Indian Springs Hotel, built by Creek Chief William McIntosh in 1823. It no longer offers lodging, and is now operated by the Butts County Historical Society.

Leave Indian Springs and continue south on GA 42. In about 5 miles, you come to the small community of Blount.

Continue on GA 42 for about a mile where you come to unpaved Stokes Store Road. The road sign is difficult to see. There is an old brick siding church at this corner. Turn left and continue on Stokes Store Rd. through farm and woodland for about 4 miles to Blue Ridge School Road, another unpaved road.

Turn right and continue to GA 83. This is a paved road. Then turn left and go about a quarter mile to US 23. Turn right (south) on US 23 and go about 3 miles, crossing the Towaliga River again, to the Juliette Road. Here you turn left and go to the small community of Juliette and the Whistle Stop Cafe, where the movie *Fried Green Tomatoes* was filmed. During the flood of July 1993, this small community was under several feet of water. Happily, it and the other shops in Juliette are in full operation again. The Juliette Grist

Drive 18: Piedmont Loop
High Falls, Indian Springs, Juliette

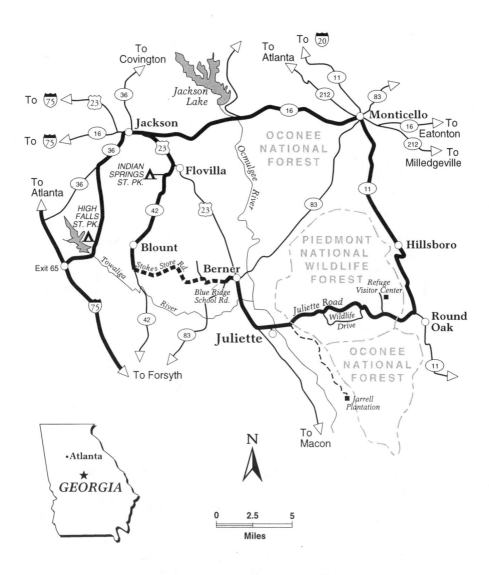

Mill, across the railroad tracks from the shops, was built in 1927. At one time it was considered the world's largest water-powered grist mill.

Leave Juliette and go east, across the railroad tracks and the bridge over the Ocmulgee River, past the community of East Juliette. In about 3 miles you come to the road on the right, which leads to the Jarrell Plantation. This road is paved for about 200 yards and is unpaved for about 3 miles to the Jarrell Plantation State Historic Site. An original middle Georgia plantation with twenty buildings dating from 1847 to 1945, this is one of the largest and most complete collections of original family artifacts of early plantation life in Georgia. There are special annual events including sheep shearing, spinning and weaving, cane grinding, and syrup making.

Backtrack to Juliette Road and turn right (east), and you enter the Piedmont National Wildlife Refuge. In about 2 miles you cross Falling Creek; shortly, you will see the entrance to the Little Rock Wildlife Drive on the right.

This is a 6-mile unpaved road that passes ponds with wood ducks, beaver, and other wetland-inhabiting wildlife. There are planted fields that provide food for wildlife. You are apt to see white-tailed deer, turkeys, both fox and gray squirrels, many kinds of birds, and a variety of wildlife habitat types from field and forests to bottomland hardwoods. A brochure available at the entrance describes the drive at a dozen stops.

The drive returns to the Juliette Road about 1.5 miles farther east. Turn right and continue east for about another 2 miles to the paved road that leads to the Refuge Headquarters and Visitor Center.

Turn left. This road forks in about a mile: the right fork leads to the visitor center, and the left to a dead end at the walk to Allison Lake. An information sign here describes some of the features of the area. Hiking trails lead to the unique nest cavities and colony site of the endangered red-cockaded woodpecker and to Allison Lake with a wildlife observation blind on the lake.

During early spring, dogwood trees are in full bloom throughout the woods of the wildlife refuge. In the fall, the hardwood trees are ablaze with autumn color. Carefully managed hunts are conducted for deer, turkey, and small game in season. Spring and fall also mark the time for many migratory birds to use the refuge for rest and feeding stops or to spend the winter.

Backtracking again to the Juliette Road, turn left and continue for about 3 miles to Georgia Highway 11. A State Forestry Department fire tower is at this intersection.

As you travel north on GA 11, you pass through a land that has seen small row-crop, subsistence farms erode away when the soils did not provide enough income to support a family. Nowadays, there are cattle farms, pine plantings that are twenty to fifty years old, and mixed hardwood forests. In about 5 miles you come to the small community of Hillsboro; a historic site, it was the home of Senator Harvey Hill of Civil War and post-Civil War fame.

The rolling topography continues for another 10 miles to the thriving town of Monticello. The Forest Service district office for Oconee National Forest is here. GA 11 travels in and out of parcels of Oconee National Forest land. Monticello is a town of tree-lined streets with dogwoods blooming in

Butts County courthouse in Jackson, a National Historic Landmark.

early spring. The antebellum and Victorian houses appear today as stately southern mansions and tastefully restored homes. A short tour of the town is worthwhile.

To complete this loop-drive, leave Monticello on GA 16 going west about 16 miles to Jackson. Again you are in and out of the national forest, farms, and private forested lands. About halfway to Jackson, you cross the Ocmulgee River just downstream from Georgia Power Company's hydropower dam impounding Jackson Lake. Roads on either side of the bridge lead up to and beyond the dam and to the lake.

The river from here to several miles downstream tumbles over a series of shoals and falls and becomes one of the most attractive streams in the state. Unfortunately, there are no easily traveled roads and only a few dirt roads that get you close enough to see the river. The Oconee National Forest borders the east bank of the river all the way down to Piedmont National Wildlife Refuge. Jackson Lake above the dam offers good fishing for largemouth bass, crappie, bluegills, and other pan fish.

From the Ocmulgee River bridge, continue west on GA 16 to Jackson, about 8 miles, to complete the loop. From Jackson, it is about 8 miles to I-75.

If you have not already taken time to see more of Jackson, you may want to spend time here. The Dauset Trail Nature Center is a well-managed private environmental center that includes hiking trails, ecology programs, plant and tree identification, and wildflower programs.

High Falls State Park.

19

Kaolin Loop
Macon, Sandersville, Milledgeville, Forsyth

General description: This 150-mile drive makes an open loop to the east from Macon at Interstate 16 to Sandersville, returning to Interstate 75 about 30 miles north of Macon. You follow just south of the Fall Line at the edge of the Upper Coastal Plain. Here sandy-clay deposits have been eroded into ridges and valleys with considerable relief. The hardwood and pine forests include a wide variety of flowering trees remarkable in spring, and offer splendid leaf color in the fall. The kaolin mines are open clay pits from which this chalky white ore is taken. Views from the ridgetops give you a perspective of the countryside. Small communities dot the drive with interesting colloquial values and history.

Special attractions: Kaolin mines located all along the drive; Macon's Ocmulgee National Monument interpreting 12,000 years of American Indian culture, and Fort Benjamin Hawkins; antebellum homes in Clinton; the 1706 trading post site on an Indian trail in Irwinton; plus fall leaf color, spring flowers, and vistas from sandy-clay ridges along a pleasant series of rural roads.

Location: Middle Georgia east of Macon.

Drive route numbers: Interstate 16; Emory Highway; U.S. Highway 80; Georgia Highways 57, 68, 272, and 24 Spur; Deepstep Road; Georgia Highways 24, 22, and 18; and U.S. Highway 129. The drive ends at Interstate 75.

Travel season: Throughout the year. Fall and spring are colorful. Winter provides better viewing of the surrounding countryside from the low ridges because the leaves fall off the deciduous trees. Kaolin operations are year-round and the historical points of interest are available all year. Tourist travel is minimal with no season of concentration. The Kaolin Festival in Sandersville begins the first Saturday in October.

Camping: Very little camping opportunity on this drive. The Forest Service recreation area on the Oconee National Forest 15 miles north of Milledgeville has fine camping facilities during the warm months, but is closed in winter. High Falls and Indian Springs state parks north of Forsyth have tent, trailer, and RV camping and cabins.

Services: Food and lodging are available at Macon, Sandersville, Milledgeville, and Forsyth.

Nearby attractions: Piedmont National Wildlife Refuge; the Macon Cherry Blossom Festival in early spring; and High Falls and Indian Springs state parks.

 The drive

Don't let the name of this drive make you think this is a trip to strip mines. In fact, it is difficult to actually get to most of the pits from which the kaolin is mined. There is much more to see along this rather long drive, including American Indian history and early colonial homes.

The drive begins in Macon at Exit 2 from I-16. From this exit, travel east on Emory Highway (Georgia Highway 19). Very shortly, U.S. Highways 129 and 80 join Emory Hwy. Stay on US 80 as you pass through the business area. In about a mile, you will pass the reconstructed Fort Hawkins on the left. This was an early crossroad trading post for Indians and predates most white settlement in the area. Fort Hawkins was built in 1806 and garrisoned by U.S. troops guarding against attacks by tribes of the Creek Confederation, particularly during the War of 1812.

Another 0.5 mile farther on US 80, you come to the entrance to Ocmulgee National Monument. This National Park Service site has about a half dozen mounds built between A.D. 900 and 1,100 by the people known as the Mississippians. There are about 6 miles of trails that connect all the archaeological and natural history features. More than 10,000 years of human use is interpreted on the grounds. The visitor center houses a major archaeological museum. You can drive to the most important points of interest on a well-designed system of park roads.

Back on US 80, turn right and continue for about 3 miles to GA 57, where you turn to the east. The road is in a section of rolling hills with dozens of open kaolin mines scattered about. Few, if any, are visible from the road because of the hardwood-pine forest. The most obvious evidence of the mining activity are the powdery white wheel marks left by heavy trucks hauling kaolin ore, usually where a dirt road enters GA 57 from the side. Kaolin is a chalk white clay material used in a wide variety of products, ranging from fine porcelain to paper, rubber, and medicine. The word kaolin comes from China and literally means "high hill," referring to the site in China from which the first white clay was sent to Europe. The making of fine china was its first use. Today, the clay is used mostly as a filler for making the glossy paper on which magazines and other "slick" publications are printed.

Most of the clay pits in this part of the drive are on the south side of the highway; there are dozens of them.

GA 57 follows along the crest of a ridge left by the erosion of the sandy clay soil over geologic time. The vantage point of the ridge affords a view of the surrounding ridges and valleys. The great variety of tree species makes this area quite colorful in the fall. If you are on this drive during the sum-

Drive 19: Kaolin Loop
Macon, Sandersville, Milledgeville, Forsyth

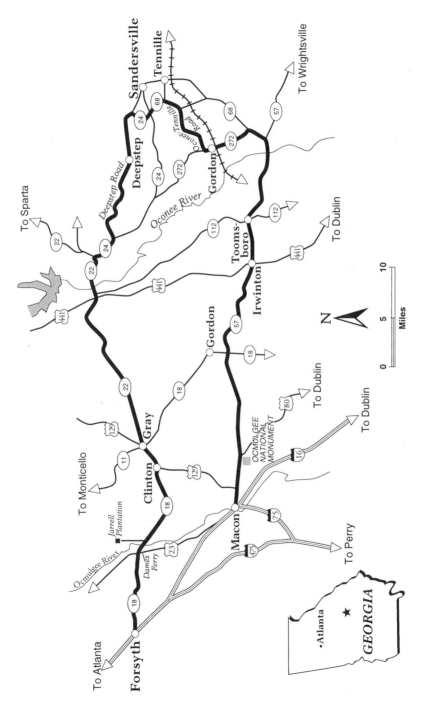

mer, look for large bushel-sized flower clusters atop a 8- to 10-foot stalk. This is the plant called "devil's walkingstick" or "Hercules' club." The flowers are creamy white, and the main stalk is covered with hundreds of sharp thorns, hence the local names. By mid-September, the cluster is a mass of dark red berries. In spring, dogwoods, redbuds, azaleas, and other flowering plants are prominent in this woodland. Reindeer lichen can be seen along the roadbanks, evidence of the sandy, well-drained soils. This area is referred to as the Fall Line sandhills.

After about 12 miles, you cross GA 18. This crossing is a few miles south of the small town of Gordon, which is one of the main shipping points for kaolin, and there is a light, white dusting of clay over the town and surrounding area. As you continue along the ridge, you get occasional vistas of the surrounding valleys and ridges. Views are much clearer in winter when the leaves are off the trees.

About 10 miles farther, you begin a gentle descent before you get to Irwinton, the county seat of Wilkinson County. Cross U.S. Highway 441 and Georgia Highway 29, which goes between Milledgeville and Dublin. This crossroad was the site of an English trading post that was in use before 1715. The old covered well, the courthouse, and the old brick church across the highway with shaded picnic area are well worth a stop and visit. From here the road remains along the ridge crest for about 7 miles, until you get to Toomsboro where Georgia Highway 112 crosses. Turn left to go into the small town, home to the Swampland Opera House performance hall. Country, gospel, and bluegrass music shows are held here every Saturday.

Back on GA 57, continue east for about 8 miles and come to the Oconee River at Ball's Ferry. Along the way, you will pass through low sandy ridges covered by dwarfed turkey oaks and other plants that can tolerate the well-drained, infertile, sandy soils. Just before you cross the bridge over the Oconee River, there is a monument and historical marker explaining that the Upper Uchee Indian Trail crossed the river at a ford just downstream. The trail was used until the ferry was built in 1816. River crossings were important in the early development of the region, and this one especially so, since it is one of the few available crossing points in an extensive swamp that borders both sides of the river for many miles. The Ball's Ferry bridge is the only view you will get of this swamp, which is as much as 4 miles wide at some points.

From the bridge, continue east on GA 57 about 3 miles to GA 68. Turn left at this intersection at the Bee Line Store. In about 3 miles, take GA 272 where it forks to the left.

Along the road are chinaberry trees growing singly or in small clumps at old abandoned house sites and along the fencerows. This tree has an attractive and fragrant lavender flower cluster. The leaves turn yellow in fall; the berries are yellow when ripe and are said to have been used by Jesuit priests to make rosaries, hence another common name, "rosary tree." This

Asian introduction was widely planted throughout the South as an ornamental, providing shade around farm homes, a use which led to still another common name, "umbrella tree." Don't eat the berries, though; they are poisonous to humans. However, blue jays are very fond of eating the overripe, fermented berries and get intoxicated from them.

In about 3 miles, you cross the Central Railroad of Georgia tracks at the small community of Oconee. Continue for about 2 miles, and turn right on Oconee-Tennille Road. This is an area of abandoned farms, pastures, planted pine forests, and reclaimed clay pits. Travel about 8 miles to GA 68. Turn left and go about 4 miles to GA 24, a divided highway. Cross GA 24 to pick up GA 24 Spur. Follow this spur for about 2.5 miles where it ends at Deepstep Road, and then turn left. This takes you around the west side of Sandersville without driving through the town.

If you would like to go into Sandersville, take GA 15 from Tennille or GA 24 . The Kaolin Festival, a week-long arts and crafts extravaganza, begins on the first Saturday in October. A driving tour of the historic features

One of two buildings in Deepstep.

of the town is described in a brochure available from the Washington County Museum or the Sandersville Chamber of Commerce.

Our drive continues on Deepstep Road. In about 3 miles, you will see the Kentucky-Tennessee Clay Company facility on the left. This is where raw kaolin is collected under large sheds and processed into a semi-liquid slurry for shipment by railroad tanker car to other parts of the country. About 2 miles farther, you come to the quaint, small town of Deepstep. A restaurant and two stores make up the entire business section of town. If you are here at lunchtime, this is a good place to stop for country cooking.

About 9 miles farther on Deepstep Road, you come to O'Quinn's Mill, which was built shortly after 1800 by Colonel Thaddus Holt. This is not a registered historic site, but it will take you back a few years to see the old building, with many of the tools still hanging on the walls and the mill dam on a picturesque stream right beside the road.

You are now in Baldwin County and about 1.5 miles from the intersection with GA 24. Continue on GA 24 to the right for about 3.5 miles and you reach GA 22. Another 3.5 miles takes you to the outskirts of Milledgeville and the bridge across Oconee River. Stay on GA 22 through Milledgeville. The special scenic and historic features of this town are discussed in Drive 17. If you have not taken that drive, you may want to stop here to see the Old State Capitol, Lockerly Arboretum, or any of several other interesting places.

Milledgeville is on the Antebellum Trail, which goes from Macon, through here, to Madison, and on to Athens. This trail was designed to show the romance and beauty of the Old South in the preserved homes, magnolia-shaded formal gardens, and history of the region.

On GA 22 west of Milledgeville, you are on the edge of the Piedmont and Fall Line regions, where there are small farms and extensive pastureland, planted pine forests, and dairies. About 10 miles from the outskirts of Milledgeville, go by Haddock. In another 6 miles you come to the town of Gray and pick up US 129 and GA 18. This 3-mile section of divided highway takes you to Clinton, where GA 18 turns to the right.

A block to the right of US 129, Clinton is truly antebellum. Located on the old road between Milledgeville and Fort Hawkins at Macon, Clinton was once the seat of Jones County, and a manufacturing center. The railroad bypassed the town, and it then dwindled in importance, its narrow streets and old homes remaining much as they had been in the early 1800s. The Old Clinton Historic District is depicted on an information sign by the road, across from the old Methodist Church. Twelve houses built between 1808 and 1830, along with the church, which was built in 1821, are still standing. Most are occupied as private residences and are kept in original appearance as near as possible. It will take an hour or more just to drive around to most of the homes on streets that have hardly changed in over a century. The big

Raw kaolin is trucked to sheds for processing and shipped as a slurry in railroad tank cars.

annual event here is Old Clinton War Days, the first weekend in May, featuring tours and Civil War reenactments.

Continue on US 129 past Clinton to GA 18 going west to the Ocmulgee River. In about 10 miles, just before you get to the river, you will see a sign for the Jarrell Plantation. A paved road leads to this historic landmark, discussed in Drive 18. The Piedmont National Wildlife Refuge and Oconee National Forest are to the north. GA 18 borders the forest before crossing the river. Across the river is the community of Dames Ferry, then you cross US 23. Lake Juliette and Rum Creek Wildlife Management Area are north of GA 18. This is also the location for Georgia Wildlife Resources' Non-Game Program office. About 10 more miles westward on GA 18 brings you to Forsyth and I-75. I-75 north goes to Atlanta, and south takes you to Macon to close the loop.

Drive 20: Pine Mountain and Callaway Gardens Loop

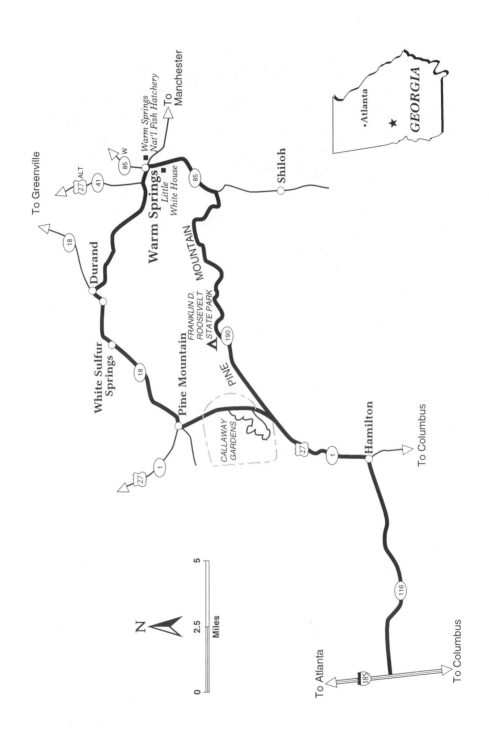

20

Pine Mountain and Callaway Gardens Loop

General description: A 56-mile drive that takes you along Pine Mountain, through Callaway Gardens, Warm Springs, and the interesting area around this southernmost mountain in Georgia.

Special attractions: Pine Mountain, a unique ridge made of quartzite rock formations, provides vistas of the Piedmont to the north and the Coastal Plain to the south, both of which are relatively flat. Callaway Gardens is a first-class resort famous for its large collection of azaleas and other flowering shrubs and trees. Cecil B. Day Butterfly Center in Callaway Gardens is the world's largest glass-enclosed butterfly conservatory. Warm Springs is the site of the geothermal springs that offered President Franklin D. Roosevelt polio therapy, the Little White House, and the National Fish Hatchery. Activities at Franklin D. Roosevelt State Park include hiking, camping, and nature study.

Location: West-central Georgia near Columbus.

Drive route numbers: Georgia Highways 116, 190, 85, 194, and 18 and U.S. Highway 27.

Travel season: Spring is the best time to see the great variety of flowering plants in gardens and yards. In summer, activities for children and adults at Callaway Gardens reach a peak. Fall foliage is outstanding most years. Weather conditions do not prevent this from being a fine winter drive.

Camping: Franklin D. Roosevelt State Park has cabins, plus tent and trailer camping. There are several commercial campgrounds in and around the city of Pine Mountain and Callaway Gardens.

Services: Lodging and food are available in Pine Mountain, Warm Springs, and at Callaway Gardens.

Nearby attractions: Fort Benning Military Reservation and the National Infantry Museum; West Point Lake and Dam; Sprewell Bluff on The Flint River near Thomaston; and Pine Mountain Wild Animal Park.

 The drive

This loop drive is only a little over 50 miles long, but it could take you at least a couple of days to fully enjoy it. The Callaway Gardens alone offer beaches, swimming, tennis courts, golf courses, vegetable and flower gardens, hiking, bicycling, canoes, paddle boats, fishing, quail hunting, dining, and live entertainment. Warm Springs boasts the Little White House, Warm Springs Foundation, shopping in the village of Warm Springs, and the federal Warm Springs Regional Fisheries Center. The city of Pine Mountain has a multitude of shops and restaurants, and just north of town is Pine Mountain Wild Animal Park, with exotic animals from around the world. When you add to this the beautiful scenery along the route, including the drive along the crest of Pine Mountain, it is a very full trip indeed.

The Pine Mountain Ridge dominates the horizon in this section—rocky, quartzite-capped, covered with longleaf pine and blackjack oak, a dramatic heights rising above the lower Piedmont. It stretches nearly 50 miles from the Chattahoochee River above Columbus to near Barnesville. It is the same ridge cut by the Flint River at Sprewell Bluff (see Drive 21). Many springs flow out of these hills. These include mineral therapeutic waters such as White Sulfur Springs, Chalybeate Springs, and most famous, Warm Springs.

Dominating the history of the area is Franklin Delano Roosevelt. The thirty-second President came here seeking ease from his polio at Warm Springs, and made his second home at the Little White House. He is said to have formulated many of the New Deal programs after seeing the problems of the local people.

The drive begins on GA 116 at its intersection with Interstate 185. Go east on GA 116. This is the foot of the Pine Mountain Ridge. The road rises and falls through the woods, scarcely broken by the occasional home. A fence beginning on the left enclosing tall hemlock trees marks Blue Springs, the private estate of the Callaway family. This was the home of textile magnate Cason J. Callaway and his wife, Virginia. The Callaways restored thousands of acres of worn-out farmland to verdant forest and productive agricultural use. Callaway Gardens, 14,000 acres of showplace gardens, is a tribute to Cason Callaway's mother, Ida Cason Callaway. Hamilton, 9 miles from I-185, is the seat of Harris County. It is a sleepy community with a lovely downtown and interesting shops appealing to travelers.

Turn left onto US 27, going north. US 27, running from Michigan to Florida, was a major north-south artery before the interstate highways were built. It now appeals to travelers who like its slower, less crowded pace. Here the highway begins the climb up the south slope of Pine Mountain Ridge. This rocky land climbs to the Callaway Gardens Country Store, first outpost of Callaway Gardens. Turn right in front of the store onto GA 190. This is the Pine Mountain Scenic Highway. Its route was personally selected by President Roosevelt. Finished in 1938, it follows the top of the ridge for 11 miles.

Franklin D. Roosevelt State Park, which you enter in a bit over a mile, was largely built by the Civilian Conservation Corps. Its 10,000 acres feature camping, swimming in a Liberty-Bell-shaped pool, and hiking on the 23-mile-long Pine Mountain Trail, one of Georgia's most popular walking sites. The road curls through a forest of short blackjack oaks, other hardwoods, and pines. There are overlooks with views north over the green forests stretching past Callaway Gardens toward Greenville and LaGrange, and south over the Pine Mountain Valley to Shiloh and the hills beyond. About 8.5 miles up the highway, a spur road leads to the right for a mile to Dowdell's Knob. This south-facing point, hundreds of feet above the valley below, was Roosevelt's favorite picnic spot. Modern travelers may also dine here at one of several tables provided.

Two and a half miles past the Dowdell's Knob turnoff, turn left at the intersection of GA 190 and GA 85. This will take you past a television transmission tower to your left. The land here was part of Roosevelt's 2,200-acre farm. It devoted 150 acres to fruits, vegetables, and livestock; the rest was pine and hardwood forest.

GA 85 descends the north face of the ridge, and near the bottom on the left, is the entrance to the Little White House Historic Site. It features a museum, gift shop, and the small cottage that was the only home Roosevelt ever owned. He died here April 12, 1945, and the house is kept the way it was that day.

At the bottom of the ridge, the town of Warm Springs has dozens of quaint antique stores, gift shops, and restaurants. The old hotel is now a bed and breakfast inn. To the right, U.S. Highway 27 Alternate leads to the Warm

Cecil B. Day Butterfly Center, the world's largest glass-enclosed butterfly conservatory, at Callaway Gardens.

Springs Regional Fisheries Center. This federal facility has a fish hatchery, visitor center, and aquarium of freshwater species.

To the left, US 27 Alt. goes past the entrance to the Warm Springs Foundation, which still is active in physical therapy. To the left beyond the Foundation entrance is the original therapy pool fed by an 87-degree thermal spring. Currently with cracked walls and a run-down bath house, it is now in the process of being restored by the state with private donations.

Turn left on GA 194, toward Durand. Go about 6 miles to the intersection with GA 18, and turn left. In 1.5 miles, you can see the crumbling remains of White Sulfur Springs. This, like Warm Springs, was a turn-of-the-century spa with mineral waters. Like most others, it faded as the twentieth century progressed.

Continue on GA 18 to the city of Pine Mountain. Then, turn left onto US 27.

A side trip here would be to turn right, follow US 27 north of town, then turn left on Oak Grove Road to Pine Mountain Wild Animal Park. Within its fences, camels, giraffes, zebras, and hundreds of other exotic animals walk free. There is a bus or driving tour through the enclosure, plus a walking area where you may touch the tamer animals.

Going south on US 27, the route is a practically constant array of shops, motels, restaurants, and gas stations from here to Callaway Gardens, a mile away. The first entrance is the Robin Lake gate, leading right to the beach, pavilion, and a large parking area. A mile past Robin Lake is the gardens entrance on the right. There is a 5-mile drive here, exceptionally beautiful (and popular) in April when thousands of azaleas are in bloom. The same drive is decorated with millions of lights for Christmas. And anytime of year, there is the John A. Sibley Horticultural Center, the Cecil B. Day Butterfly Center, and Mr. Cason's Vegetable Garden.

Continue south on US 27 to take you back to Hamilton, then right on GA 116 to Interstate 185. From Pine Mountain, GA 18 and US 27 North also return you to I-185.

21

Thomaston to Buena Vista

General description: This 75-mile drive takes you through the Fall Line on the western part of the state. Rolling hills and the Flint River add relief that gives the drive much character.

Special attractions: Sprewell Bluff and Flint River shoals; Flint River Outdoor Center; Big Lazer Public Fishing Area at Talbotton; and the Celebrity Collection, Elvis Presley Museum, and Front Porch Music Hall at Buena Vista.

Location: West-central Georgia.

Drive route numbers: Georgia Highways 36, 41, and 22.

Travel season: A year-round drive; winter weather is virtually never a factor to drivers in this portion of the state.

Camping: Campgrounds at Franklin D. Roosevelt State Park and at Callaway Gardens, about 30 miles west of this drive.

Services: The newly renovated, historic Hotel Upson in Thomaston. Bed and breakfasts in Thomaston and Buena Vista. Restaurants and hotel/motel accommodations in and near Columbus and Pine Mountain and at small towns along the route.

Nearby attractions: Fort Benning Military Reservation with the Infantry Museum; Callaway Gardens; Plains, with the Jimmy Carter National Historic Site; Andersonville National Historic Site; Providence Canyon State Park; and Westville, a reconstructed colonial village.

 The drive

This drive goes from the Piedmont region to the Coastal Plain. It crosses the Pine Mountain Ridge at the Flint River, continues to Woodland, turns south through Talbotton and Geneva, and ends at Buena Vista.

The northern portion of the trip follows GA 36 through hilly, rocky land, covered for the most part in oak, poplar, sweet gum, and other hardwoods. This is the Pine Mountain Ridge, a height rising between the Piedmont to the north and the Coastal Plain to the south. Here an outcropping of granite resists the wearing effects of water, forcing streams to flow over falls and rocky shoals. This Fall Line runs from Columbus, through Macon, and on to Augusta. To the Indians who lived here before European settlement, and whose paths became the early roads, the Fall Line also marked the best stream crossings. Where shoals made rivers and creeks shallow, it

Drive 21: Thomaston to Buena Vista

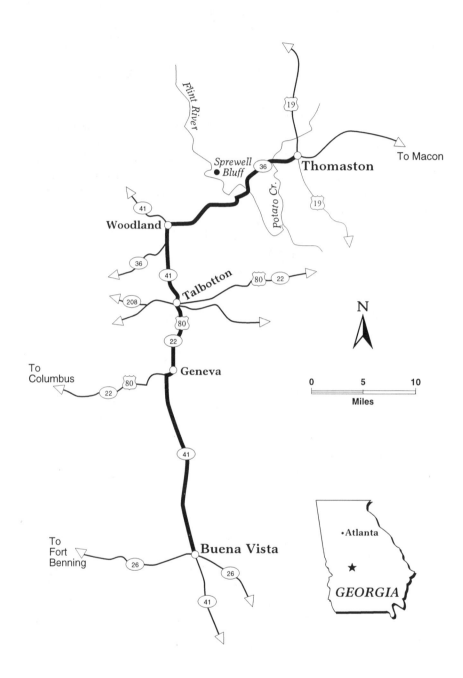

was easy to wade across them. Paths converged on these river fords, and towns grew near them. When whites arrived traveling on the paths the Indians had made, they found the Fall Line was also a source of water power. In addition, as a barrier to river navigation, the falls and shoals marked the first practical embarkation point for shipping crops and goods downstream. Settlers built their towns and factories in the same places the Indians had chosen. You can say the Fall Line is a geologic feature that shaped Georgia's history.

Activities available in this section include hiking, canoeing, and camping along the Flint River, which winds its way through the Pine Mountain Ridge at Sprewell Bluff. Public hunting and fishing is allowed at the Big Lazar Creek Wildlife Management Area and Big Lazar Public Fishing Area.

The southern section of the drive begins as you turn on Georgia Highway 41 at Woodland and enter the Coastal Plain. This portion of the state was sea floor in the relatively recent geological past. The hills here are more gentle, and the soil is sandy, testifying to the time when the ocean covered the land. Vegetation changes here, too. There are stands of scrub oak and loblolly pine. The pine is grown as a crop, for paper pulp. Another tree grown here is the peach. Orchards beginning near Talbotton are in colorful bloom in spring, and produce fruit in the summer months.

When you reach Buena Vista (pronounced B'you-na Vista) at the end of the drive, you will find a town dedicated to making itself an entertainment mecca. Music halls featuring big-name country stars, a museum with the largest private collection of Elvis Presley memorabilia in the country, antique and gift shops, and rodeo and motorcycle-racing venues make Buena Vista a happening place in an out-of-the-way location.

The drive starts at the courthouse square in Thomaston at the intersection of US 19 and GA 36. The Upson County Courthouse is on the National Register of Historic Places. There are also several antique shops and a movie house dating to 1920 on the square. Go west on GA 36, taking care to follow the signs as the road makes a couple of turns before it leaves town. As you leave Thomaston, you will notice you are in hill country. The road crosses Potato Creek, and to the left, you can see the stream tumbling over a steep shoal. GA 36 keeps to the ridge crest, affording glimpses of far countryside and hills through the trees. Three miles past Potato Creek, turn right at the caution light at Roland, toward Flint River Baptist Church. You are going to Sprewell Bluff, where the Flint River cuts through the Pine Mountain Ridge in a very uncharacteristic (for this part of the country) display of whitewater. Two miles down the road, turn left on Old Alabama Road. This early trading path led from Athens to Columbus, and crossed the Flint by ferry. The ferry was replaced by two bridges, spanning the stream downstream at Owens Island. There is no river crossing on this road now. As you ride along the ridge crest you will pass a clearcut to the left and, 0.5 mile later, an older clearcut site, replanted with pines. Clearcutting is a forestry practice in which all the trees in a stand are cut down. Usually, clearcuts are replanted with pine trees. One advantage of the practice is that it opens up the view here giving a wide vista to the south and east, showing hills, ridges, water towers, and so forth, all the way back to Thomaston.

You will start seeing turnoffs on the right, and paths leading into the woods, leading to the ridge edge overlooking the Flint River several hundred feet below. The road winds down the hillside and you arrive at Sprewell Bluff on the river. This is a high granite bluff on the far side of the Flint. Growing on it are mountain laurel and rhododendron. These plants are native to the Appalachian highlands, the kind of things you would expect to see in the North Georgia Mountains. Beginning in the 1930s, the U.S. Army Corps of Engineers was authorized to study building a hydroelectric dam across the river at Sprewell Bluff. The Georgia Power Company later intended to carry out this project, but the plan to drown this scenic area was opposed by conservation groups, and was eventually dropped during the Presidency of Georgia's Jimmy Carter. The state now owns 1,200 acres around the site, and is in the process of making improvements to the accommodations. At this writing, the park consists of picnic tables, a large gravel parking area, and a boat ramp. It is popular with locals for picnics, fishing, and floating down the river, especially in the summer. Hunting for deer, turkey, and small game is allowed in season. The Flint River originates in Atlanta, is channeled under the Atlanta airport, and joins the Chattahoochee River at Lake Seminole in southwest Georgia near Bainbridge. There the two rivers become the Apalachicola River, emptying into the Gulf of Mexico.

On the way back to GA 36, your right turn is at the Angus farm sign. Then, turn right at the blinking caution light, back onto GA 36. Two miles later, just over the bridge, is the Flint River Outdoor Center. This business offers shuttle and rental service for canoeing and tubing on the river, as well as camping.

Beyond the river another mile, Old Alabama Road joins the highway from the left. A historic marker alludes to the river crossing at Double Bridges and to a Civil War skirmish there a week after Lee's surrender at Appomatox. Continue past the community of Pleasant Hill, and enter Woodland. This small community consists of a tiny business district of brick storefronts. It is a community that has suffered from the migration from farms to cities. This is even more apparent after you turn left across the railroad tracks onto GA 41 and head south. There is an abandoned brick school building on the left, of 1930s or 1940s vintage. A short distance later, Jeff Hendricks Road bears off to the left, and on it is another 1950s-era school, also abandoned. Continue straight on GA 41, 6 miles to Talbotton. The seat of Talbot County, Talbotton was founded in 1827, the year the Creek Confederation "ceded" its land to the United States in return for a land grant in Arkansas. The

Sprewell Bluff on Flint River near Thomaston.

Creek tribes were great rivals of the Cherokees to the north, and fought long and bitter wars for territory. Later, the Creeks fought white settlers moving here, and sided with the British during the War of 1812. General Andrew Jackson carried on a campaign against them with the aid of the Cherokees. A portion of these proud people moved south to Florida, called themselves the Seminole, or Outlaws, and continued raids on Georgia settlements until 1838.

Just past the junction with US 80, there is a marker pointing to the site of the Straus home. Lazarus Straus immigrated to America from Bavaria and settled in Talbotton, where he started a mercantile business. After the Civil War, he moved to New York City and began a store that became Macy's.

Continue on to the very fine old church on the left. This is Zion Episcopal Church. It was built in 1848, and has not been modernized. It has a bellows-operated pipe organ that has been in regular use since it was installed in 1850. There is also a marker here noting the passage of the noted naturalist William Bartram, who traveled this area in the mid-eighteenth century.

To the east of Talbotton, Big Lazar Creek Wildlife Management Area and Big Lazar Public Fishing Area is a state-run hunting and fishing site, offering managed hunts for deer, turkey, and small game in season, and fishing for catfish, bluegill, and bass in a stocked lake. To reach it, go east 4 miles on US 80 to Po Biddy Crossroads, turn left and follow Po Biddy Road

6.5 miles to Bunkham Road. Turn left (beyond Collinsworth Methodist Church) on this dirt road, which leads you into the WMA.

South of Talbotton, the character of the land changes to gently rolling hills marking the start of the Coastal Plain. You will begin to see peach orchards with trees arranged in neat rows. In early spring, these hills look as if they are covered with a beautiful pink mist as the peaches come into bloom.

As you continue south on GA 41 through Geneva, the roadside soil is no longer Georgia red clay, but sand. This is ancient seacoast, and these hills were once dunes. The area is naturally covered with scrubby turkey oaks and longleaf pines. In recent years, the land has been planted in stands of loblolly pine for the pulp and timber industry.

Eight miles south of Geneva, a historic marker indicates the route of the Old Federal Road. Before that, it was the Lower Creek Trading Path, when this was Indian territory. In 1805, the United States got permission from the Creeks to open this road that ran from Fort Hawkins, where Macon is now, to the Alabama River above Mobile, Alabama. Ironically, when relations with the white man turned sour and war broke out in 1813, the route the Indians granted was used by army troops who built a strongpoint called Fort Perry near here.

In about 3 miles, the road passes a series of long, low buildings. These are chicken houses. They house thousands of birds that are raised to market size in a few weeks, then shipped out to processing houses. Georgia is one of the nation's top poultry producers. The chicken industry is more associated with north Georgia around Gainesville, but there are a number of houses here.

Most of the towns since Thomaston have been sleepy, but Buena Vista is wide awake, and determined to make itself a center of tourism and entertainment. As you follow GA 41 into the downtown square, you'll see antique and gift shops, an Elvis Presley museum, and cafes. There are also a couple of music halls: one in town, and a larger one 4 miles south on GA 41. These feature big-name country music stars in weekend shows.

An unusual site just northwest of town is Pasaquan, the home and studio of the late Eddie Owens Martin, who called himself Saint Eom. This visionary artist built his home into a mystical environment with colorfully painted walls and sculpted ornaments. Owned and operated by the local historical society, it is open for tours on weekends.

22

Columbus to Providence Canyon

General description: A 68-mile drive on good secondary roads leaves Columbus and travels south through the forested part of Fort Benning Military Reservation, past the little towns of Louvale and Omaha, to the Chattahoochee River impounded behind Walter F. George Dam. The route visits Florence Marina and Providence Canyon state parks before ending at historic Westville Village at Lumpkin.

Special attractions: Upper Coastal Plain sandy-clay ridges; Indian mounds; Florence Marina State Park's Kirbo Interpretive Center; Providence Canyon State Park; and Westville Historic Village with 1800s buildings and handicrafts. State parks offer fishing, camping, birding, wildlife watching, and hiking.

Location: West-central part of the state south of Columbus in the Chattahoochee River valley.

Drive route numbers: Interstate 185; U.S. Highway 27/Georgia Highway 1; and Georgia Highways 39, 39C, and 39SP.

Travel season: A year-round drive. Spring and fall are best for flowers and leaf color.

Camping: Tent, trailer, and RV camping and cabins at Florence Marina State Park.

Services: Restaurants, motels, and hotels in Columbus. Services limited except at state parks along the drive.

Nearby attractions: Walter F. George Reservoir; Fort Benning Military Reservation and Infantry Museum; Eufaula National Wildlife Refuge; Plains, Georgia, with Jimmy Carter National Historic Site; Callaway Gardens; and Franklin D. Roosevelt State Park.

 The drive

This drive starts near Columbus, the second largest city in Georgia (after Atlanta), and ends at Westville, a town of authentic structures brought to one spot and frozen in the mid-1800s. It begins south of Columbus, goes through the Fort Benning Military Reservation to Cusseta, then west to Omaha on the Chattahoochee River, south to Florence Landing State Park, west to Providence Canyon State Park, and on to Lumpkin and Westville. The geography and geology of the land is important here; this is the transition between the Piedmont and the Coastal Plain. The region is called the

Drive 22: Columbus to Providence Canyon

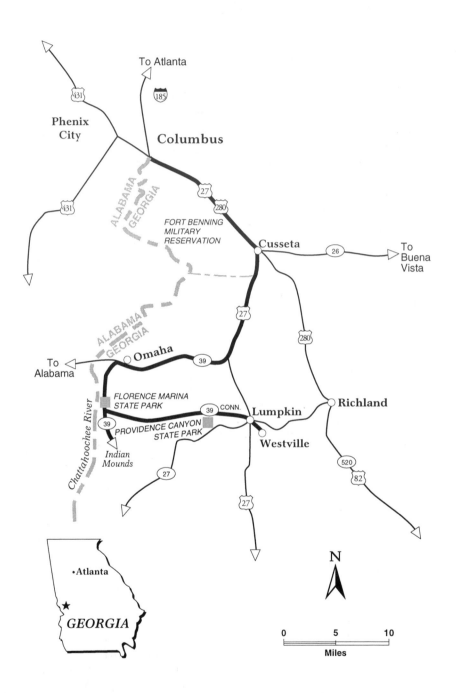

Fall Line, because granite outcroppings running across the central part of the state from Columbus to Macon and Augusta make shoals and waterfalls on the streams. At Providence Canyon, the land is much more vulnerable to running water, and deep gullies have formed there in the 175 years since settlers started farming the area.

Shoals on the Chattahoochee that made the river easy to cross made the area a focal point for Indian trading paths and early roads. Where the roads converged, towns grew. The area has been an important center of population for hundreds of years. The Kashita tribe of the Creek Confederation lived here at Kashita Town, first near the present day Columbus, and later at what is now called Cusseta. Hernando de Soto came here on his expedition through the Southeast in 1540; later, English merchants from Charleston arrived to barter trade goods for animal hides and furs. Pioneers traveled this way, making the river crossings their gateway to new lands in Alabama, Mississippi, and beyond. Columbus was a major commercial and industrial center, sending cotton and manufactured goods down the Chattahoochee on riverboats.

The western edge of this drive touches Lake Walter F. George, better known as Lake Eufaula.

The drive starts on US 27 at the intersection with I-185 at the south end of Columbus. Travel south on US 27.

A side trip via I-185 South takes you to the Main Post of Fort Benning. There are a number of attractions at Fort Benning, including the Infantry Museum, and the firing ranges of the Army Marksmanship Training Unit, which has produced a large number of Olympic medalists in the shooting sports. Fort Benning, established during World War I, now covers 182,000 acres and is one of the world's largest military reservations. It is home to the Infantry School, Airborne Training School, Ranger School, School of the Americas, Army Marksmanship Unit, and Army Physical Fitness School. The reservation is also an economic dividing line: to the north, Columbus is bustling and prosperous; south of Fort Benning, Chattahoochee and Stewart counties are two of Georgia's poorest. The soil here was depleted by intensive cotton farming in the last century, and, unable to make a living off the land, many farmers sold out to timber and paper companies. What once was an area of small farms is now a region of pine plantations.

Along US 27 are a number of military facilities on either side of the highway. You are on the Fort Benning Reservation practically all the way to Cusseta, and can expect to see troops and army vehicles along the way, even the occasional tank or Bradley Fighting Vehicle. Known as Victory Drive, this four-lane concrete road was built during World War II to facilitate movement of troops and equipment. It still does so a half century later. Pine and oak forest borders much of the road. It is home to a large population of wildlife, including many white-tailed deer. These animals can often be seen

Providence Canyon State Park.

browsing on the roadside, particularly in the evening hours and at dawn and dusk. Exercise caution, for they often bolt onto the highway without warning.

Continue on US 27 at Cusseta. This community was known as Kashita Town to the Creek Indians. The original townsite is on the grounds of the commanding general's headquarters at Fort Benning near the Chattahoochee River. However, it was burned by the Spanish in 1686. Eventually the town relocated here. It is pronounced "Ca-SEE-tuh." South of Cusseta, the terrain is marked by the hills and valleys of the upper Coastal Plain. This was once below the surface of the ocean. You do not see many homes or other signs of human habitation in this vicinity, and Stewart and Chattahoochee counties are sparsely populated for a couple of reasons. First, the Fort Benning reservation covers much of it; second, the land was worn out by poor farming methods, and small landowners have largely been replaced by large timber and paper companies who have planted the area with pine trees.

Nine miles from Cusseta is Louvale. This tiny community is notable for its "church row." There are four buildings resting in the shade of giant oak trees on the right. Three of the buildings are churches, and one used to be. They are the Antioch Baptist, Antioch Methodist, Antioch Institute, and Antioch Primitive Baptist—the town was called Antioch until 1886. Antioch Institute was a school until the 1940s, and is now the scene of an annual "sacred harp" singing convention. Sacred harp or shaped-note singing is done a cappella, with the singers reading the notes by their shapes in special songbooks, and is an old Southern method of church singing not practiced much anymore.

South of Louvale, the road crosses Hannahatchee Creek. Many streams here retain their Indian names. The "-hatchee" suffix attached to them means creek or river. A mile past the creek, turn right onto GA 39. A sign indicates that this is the way to Florence Marina State Park and Kirbo Outdoor Education Center.

Near Omaha, a historic marker indicates an Indian trail passed through this way to Oconee Village, 3 miles away. The Oconees, part of the Creek Confederation, left here between 1750 and 1799. Thereafter known as the Seminole, they fought with white settlers until 1838, when they were driven to take refuge in Florida's Everglades.

The town of Omaha is bypassed by the highway and remains as it would have been in the 1940s or 1950s. Sitting on a bluff above the river floodplain, it includes old stores, and in the middle of the street just down from the post office, the town well. A historic marker on the highway indicates this was the site of Fort McCreary, built for defense of settlers during the Creek Indian War in 1836. Three unknown soldiers of that conflict are buried at the old fort site, a mile north.

At the intersection of GA 39 and GA 39 Spur, turn left on GA 39 (GA 39 Spur leads to a bridge over the Chattahoochee River into Alabama). The road now runs in the river floodplain, and there is more farming here. As you cross creekbottoms, you will start to see Spanish moss hanging from trees like gray beards. This plant is not a parasite on the trees, but rather lives on nutrients in the air. This is about as far north as you will find Spanish moss in the Chattahoochee Valley.

If you should take this drive in the wintertime, you can see mistletoe growing on hardwoods, particularly oak. It grows in green clusters on the tree limbs, and is very visible when the trees lose their foliage. Mistletoe is a parasite, drawing nutrients from the host tree.

Four miles from Omaha is Florence Marina State Park. There was once a town and a bridge across the river here, but the bridge washed away in a flood and the town faded away. Today the park sits on the shore of the Walter F. George Reservoir (Lake Eufaula) and features a marina, camping, cabins, and the Kirbo Outdoor Educational Center. The center features artifacts of the old town, as well as of the Indians who lived here originally.

At the entrance to Florence Marina State Park, GA 39 Connector heads east off GA 39. Take this road toward Providence State Park. When you start climbing out of the river plain, you will begin to see eroded gullies. Farmers who plowed this land for fields cut through the protective clay, opening the sandy subsoil to the elements. The moundlike hills on the left are the result of the soil wearing away. Erosion was worst at what is now Providence

Canyon State Park. The entrance is on the right, 10 miles from Florence Marina. Erosion began in the 1830s when the first white settlers plowed this land. Now what began as gullies are canyons over 150 feet deep. Forty-three different varieties of sandy subsoil color the canyon walls in a multitude of pastel pinks, blues, yellows, and whites. The rugged walls and pinnacles of this man-caused natural wonder inspired the title "Georgia's Little Grand Canyon." The park features a small museum, picnic areas, and trails into the canyons. Primitive camping is allowed, but you must register with the park office.

Six miles past Providence Canyon on GA 39 Conn., you come to Lumpkin. Turn left onto GA 27 and enter downtown Lumpkin. The Stewart County Courthouse sits in the center of the town square, surrounded by old buildings including the turn-of-the-century Hatchett Drug Store Museum. One feature of the museum particularly welcome in the summertime is an authentic working soda fountain and ice cream parlor. On the west side of the square is Bedingfield Inn, a restored 1836 stagecoach inn. This private residence is open for tours each afternoon. Turn right at the sign pointing toward Westville onto Martin Luther King Boulevard and continue a mile south of Lumpkin. On the left is the entrance to Westville. This town, advertised as "Where It's Always 1850," never actually existed. However, all the buildings in it are authentic structures built before 1850. They were brought to this 58-acre site and restored to create a living history village.

Cotton bale press at Westville, a reconstucted colonial village.

One of the colonial homes preserved in Westville, "Where It's Always 1850."

Costumed interpreters and craftspeople carry on life as it was lived in the pre-Civil War era. You can see the blacksmith at his forge, the carpenter and cooper, basket weaver, and the cook at the open hearth baking (delicious!) gingerbread. It is wise to wear flat-heeled walking shoes when you visit here, since the streets, as they would have been in 1850, are unpaved and can be uneven. Special events during the year include Independence Day celebrations, Christmas observances, and the Fair of 1850 in the fall.

Drive 23: Bainbridge to Eufaula
Blakely, Kolomoki Mounds, Fort Gaines

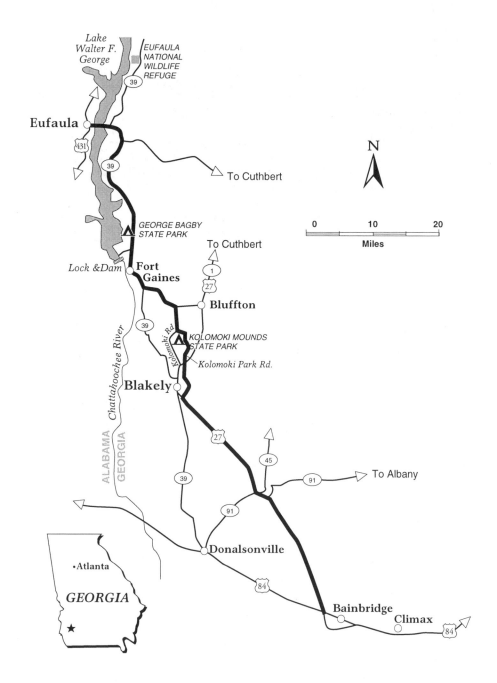

23

Bainbridge to Eufaula

Blakely, Kolomoki Mounds, Fort Gaines

General description: This is a 65-mile drive in the southwestern corner of the state. If you travel from south to north, you go from the very flat part of the Coastal Plain around Bainbridge into the red hills and sand hills of the Fall Line at Fort Gaines and Georgetown. Next, Kolomoki Mounds State Park is on the edge of the red hills region. Hardwood forests then begin to dominate the pinelands so common in the Coastal Plain.

Special attractions: Kolomoki Mounds State Park, the bluffs and views of the Chattahoochee River valley at Fort Gaines, and Fort Gaines Lock and Dam with its 88-foot lift make this a drive with much variety. George T. Bagby State Park and the U. S. Army Corps of Engineers' Cotton Hill on Lake Walter F. George both provide good access to the lake.

Location: Southwest corner of Georgia along the Chattahoochee River valley.

Drive route numbers: U.S. Highway 27/Georgia Highway 1; Georgia Highway 39; and Kolomoki Park Road.

Travel season: Year-round. Winter weather is just as good for travel as other times of the year. Late winter to early spring is best for flowers. Fall leaf color in the red hills area can be exceptional. The lakes provide good fishing for some species almost all year.

Camping: The Corps of Engineers' Cotton Hill has excellent tent, trailer, and RV campsites. Kolomoki Mounds State Park has similar facilities, although with fewer campsites. Farther north, on Lake Walter F. George, Florence Marina State Park has good camping facilities. Seminole State Park on Lake Seminole has both campsites and cottages.

Services: Motels and restaurants in Bainbridge; lodge and restaurant at George Bagby State Park; motels and restaurants at Eufaula, Alabama; gas is available in the small towns along the way.

Nearby attractions: Providence Canyon State Park; Westville, a living history village; Lake Seminole and its outstanding warmwater fishing; Eufaula National Wildlife Refuge; and Coheelee Creek Covered Bridge, 9 miles west of Blakely off Georgia Highway 62, the southernmost "kissing bridge" still standing.

The drive

This drive roughly follows the Chattahoochee River valley, from Bainbridge at Georgia's southwest corner, to Georgetown and its twin city across the river, Eufaula, Alabama. Running through the river plain, and on the Coastal Plain region, this is a generally flat route with the only suggestion of hills being at the bluffs overlooking the Chattahoochee at Fort Gaines and Eufaula. It is largely agricultural, with fields of cotton, peanuts, and soybeans stretching for miles along the roadside.

This river valley has been an avenue of commerce since the earliest Indians entered the area thousands of years ago. Signs of these early inhabitants exist today at Kolomoki Mounds State Park, which was the site of the largest Indian ceremonial center in south Georgia. Spanish explorers, soldiers, and priests were the first Europeans to travel this way in the 1600s. Then came English traders. Friction between the two developed; the Spanish and English fought each other, and the various tribes of the Creek Confederacy fought everybody, off and on, until the end of the Creek Wars in 1838. Colquitt and Fort Gaines have memorial statues honoring these fierce warriors.

Blakely has a statue to the peanut, as well as a flagpole erected in 1861 to fly the bonnie blue flag of the Confederate States of America. Colquitt is a center of production of tasty mayhaw jelly, and holds a festival for that cranberry-sized relative of the apple the third weekend in April.

River traffic still plies the Chattahoochee, as does U.S. Army Corps of Engineers, which maintains a shipping channel for barges as well as locks to move them through Woodruff, Andrews, and George dams.

The major recreational opportunities are at the impoundments behind the dams. Lake Seminole behind Jim Woodruff Dam, and Lake Walter F. George (better known as Lake Eufaula) backed up by Walter F. George Dam, are famous for the quality of their largemouth bass, striped bass, and hybrid bass fishing. Hunting, boating, water sports, and camping are popular along the shores of these large impoundments.

Drive 22, Columbus to Providence Canyon, is at the north end of this drive. The nearest interstate highway access is from I-185 at Columbus, via U.S. Highway 431 through Phoenix City, Alabama, and south to Eufaula.

The drive starts on US 27, heading north at the intersection of U.S. Highways 84 and 27, on the west side of Bainbridge. Bainbridge is located on a site that was once a frontier trading post on the Flint River. West of here, the Flint joins the Chattahoochee in Lake Seminole. The stream that emerges from Woodruff Dam is the Apalachicola River, which flows through the Florida Panhandle to the Gulf of Mexico. Lake Seminole is noted for producing lunker largemouth bass, as well as striped bass, hybrid bass, and

Replica of a blockhouse on the site of the original Fort Gaines, overlooking the Chattahoochee River below Fort Gaines Dam.

catfish. The shallow bays of the lake are also popular with duck hunters. Bainbridge prospered with rail and river traffic and is rich in Victorian and Neoclassical homes. A self-guided driving tour is available from the Bainbridge Chamber of Commerce, located in the McKensie-Reynolds House at Earle May Boat Basin Park. This park is just west of the US 84 bypass on GA 97 Connector.

Our trip uses the four-lane US 27, with its businesses and factories set well back from the road. In about 5 miles, the road narrows to two lanes, but as of this writing, construction is underway adding two more lanes; the work is scheduled to be finished by early 1997.

Continue through Eldorendo along broad, flat fields. In these fields you will see things that look like huge lawn sprinklers, which are, in fact, self-propelled irrigation sprinklers. Farmers here irrigate their fields by pumping water from deep wells through these devices. The sprinklers travel on wheels in circles a half-mile across. Critics say all the pumping for this and industrial uses is depleting the aquifer in this area; farmers and industrialists say they need the water.

Seventeen miles north of Bainbridge, is the town of Colquitt. A sign identifies Colquitt as the home of the annual Mayhaw Festival. A mayhaw is a cranberry-sized relative of the apple. The bushlike tree grows in low, swampy areas around here. Local people gather the fruit of the tree in springtime by wading into the bogs where the trees grow, spreading bedsheets under the trees, and shaking the ripe mayhaws into the sheets. Jelly mavens say that the jelly made from mayhaws is the best-tasting jelly in the world. Local stores stock the delicacy, so you may form your own opinion.

As you reach the business section of Colquitt, to the left beside the cemetery is a giant Indian head, a sculpture 12 feet high. A legend on a rock in front of the statue says it is part of "The Trail of the Whispering Giants." It is the work of Hungarian sculptor Peter Toth, who brought it here in 1973. It appears the statue was carved from wood, then coated with fiberglass. It is showing signs of decay from standing in the south Georgia weather for more than twenty years.

Cross Spring Creek, and bear right to stay on US 27. When you get to the Hentown community, there is a marker designating this the Martha Berry Highway. The full length of US 27 in Georgia honors Miss Berry, who began a school for poor mountain children at her home north of Rome, Georgia, that grew into Berry College. Drive 3 visits that school.

Blakely, seat of Early County, is 7 miles north of Hentown. You have a choice at Blakely; to follow US 27 to the right, bypassing the town, or to take US 27 Business into downtown Blakely and its courthouse square. Here, you will find the Peanut Monument which honors Georgia's number one cash crop and, on the northwest corner of the square, the last Confederate flagpole. On May 16, 1861, at the onset of the Civil War, local people cut a tall longleaf pine and hauled it here by ox team. It was set into the ground to fly the "bonnie blue flag" of the Confederacy. The flagpole is still there, although you cannot actually see it, since it is encased in a sheath of fiberglass. If you go into town, continue on US 27 Bus. to the sign indicating a left turn toward Kolomoki Mounds on Kolomoki Road. The park entrance is 5 miles up this road on the right.

Note: There are two roads to Kolomoki Mounds Park. Kolomoki Road goes to the west park entrance, and Kolomoki Park Road goes to the east park entrance. It doesn't matter which you take, since it is 5 miles to the

Modern sculpture at Colquitt, called "The Trail of the Whispering Giants."

park either way. For simplicity, we suggest taking the first road you come to that points to the mounds.

If you skipped the Peanut Monument and Confederate flagpole and bypassed Blakely, turn left onto US 27 Bus. north of town, then take the first right at the "Kolomoki Mounds State Park" sign onto Kolomoki Park Rd. Five miles up Kolomoki Park Rd. you come to the park entrance on the left.

Turn into the entrance and continue past the lake to the mounds. The park is the site of seven pre-Columbian mounds erected by the Swift Creek and Weeden Island Indians. The largest, a temple mound built in the twelfth and thirteenth centuries, is more than fifty feet high. It is one of the largest mounds in the United States. The people who built this disappeared and were replaced in the 1500s by people of the Lamar culture, who were the ancestors of the tribes forming the Creek Confederation.

The temple mound looks across a wide grassy field toward several much smaller mounds and, several hundred yards away, to the Kolomoki Mounds Museum. The museum is built into the side of a small burial mound and preserves an undisturbed archaeological excavation. In addition to the archaeological sites, the park offers fishing, boating, swimming, hiking, picnicking, and camping.

Continuing west past the museum, turn right at a T intersection onto Kolomoki Rd., which is unmarked here. Follow this road 5 miles to another T intersection and turn left. A sign indicates this is the way to George Bagby State Park.

The road here is beginning to carry you out of the Coastal Plain. The roadside dirt is tinged with red Georgia clay, and the land begins to rise more than it has done before.

In 5 miles, turn right onto GA 39. (If you are taking this trip backwards from Eufaula to Bainbridge, the unnumbered county roads are marked by signs indicating "Kolomoki Mounds State Park.") In a mile you enter the Fort Gaines city limits, but the town does not really show up for another mile or so.

In downtown Fort Gaines, turn left to continue on GA 39, go one block and turn right, still on GA 39. Go to Carroll Street and turn left. In a few blocks you cross Jackson Street and enter the parking area at the site of the original Fort Gaines, for which the town is named. It was built on this river bluff above the Chattahoochee River during the Creek Indian Wars in 1816. A replica blockhouse is on the site now, as is a "frontier village" of log buildings. During the Civil War, this was an artillery post, guarding river passage. A Confederate cannon is still mounted there. There is also another giant Indian head statue here, similar to the one in Colquitt. This one, erected in 1989, was carved by Philip Andrews. It, too, is succumbing to the rigors of outdoor exposure. An inscription says it is in honor of Otis Micco, whose

Seminole followers fled south from here rather than submit to the white man's rule. Fort Gaines was a big shipping point for cotton before the railroads were built. Bales stored in warehouses were slid down the bluff to waiting riverboats below, and from there, taken down the river to the world's markets.

Backtrack on Carroll Street and turn left onto GA 39 to head out of town. At this end of Fort Gaines, another replica blockhouse serves as a welcome sign to visitors entering town from the north.

Two miles north of Fort Gaines is the Walter F. George Dam. You can drive 1.2 miles along the earth portion of this dam to the locks and floodgate structure. The locks can raise or lower river traffic more than 80 feet from the lake above to the river below. This is the second highest lock east of the Mississippi. Watching the locks fill and empty is a very impressive sight, with the water rising rapidly in the locks, and a giant rush of water downstream as the chamber empties to the river level below. Unfortunately, there is not a steady enough volume of barge traffic to count on having a good chance to view this spectacle.

Two miles past the dam, you come to the entrance to George T. Bagby State Park. There is a thirty-room lodge here with a restaurant, as well as rental cabins, swimming beach, hiking trail, picnic sites, and a marina. Cotton Hill Campground on the left beyond Bagby Park offers a large campground and boat ramp as part of U. S. Army Corps of Engineers amenities on the lake.

At Pataula Creek, the road crosses an arm of the lake. Lake George covers 48,000 acres, and you will almost always see people fishing, no matter what time of year you visit.

Pass Pataula Park Recreation Area and continue north to the outskirts of Georgetown, where GA 39 turns left to pick up US 82. This will lead you into Georgetown.

Georgetown, Georgia, and Eufaula, Alabama, sit on either side of the Chattahoochee River. Eufaula is by far the larger and more prosperous community, with more amenities for the traveler than its Georgia sister. Crossing the river on Vandiver Causeway (US 82) will take you to Eufaula. On this side of the river you can also access the Eufaula National Wildlife Refuge and Lake Point Resort, operated by the Alabama parks system.

Drive 24: Peach Country
Georgia Highway 49 to Plains

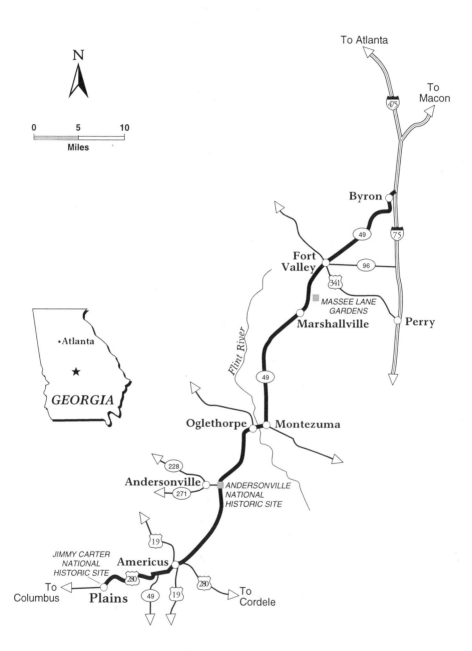

N

0 5 10
Miles

To Atlanta

To Macon

475

Byron

49

75

Fort Valley

96

341

MASSEE LANE GARDENS

Marshallville

Perry

Flint River

•Atlanta

★

GEORGIA

49

Oglethorpe

Montezuma

228

Andersonville

271

ANDERSONVILLE NATIONAL HISTORIC SITE

19

JIMMY CARTER NATIONAL HISTORIC SITE

Americus

280

To Columbus

Plains

49

19

280

To Cordele

24

Peach Country
Georgia Highway 49 to Plains

General description: This 68-mile drive passes through the heart of the peach orchard country and ends at Plains, Georgia, birthplace and home of former President Carter.

Special Attractions: Early spring peaches in bloom; midsummer peach harvest; pecan groves; peanuts; Massee Lane Gardens; Marshallville; Andersonville National Historic Site; the Jimmy Carter National Historic Site in Plains; and the town of Montezuma, displaying evidence of the flood of 1994.

Location: West-central Georgia.

Drive route numbers: Interstate 75, Georgia Highway 49, and U.S. Highway 280.

Travel season: Year-round. Early March to April for peach blossoms, azaleas, camellias, and many wildflowers and flowering trees. Peach harvest is in June. Historic sites are open year-round, and have seasonal events throughout the year.

Camping: No easily available campgrounds along this drive.

Services: Bed and breakfasts, motels, and hotels in all the towns along the drive. Good restaurants in larger towns such as Byron, Montezuma, Americus, and Plains. Consider having barbeque or other regional specialties.

Nearby attractions: Fort Benning Military Reservation and Infantry Museum; Providence Canyon State Park; George T. Bagby State Park; Georgia Veterans Memorial State Park; Whitewater Creek State Park; Ocmulgee National Monument; Warm Springs; Roosevelt's Little White House Historic Site; Pine Mountain; and Callaway Gardens.

 The drive

The peach-growing country of Georgia is in the gently rolling upper Coastal Plain. The orchards are scattered throughout this section of the state in several counties, including Crawford, Macon, Taylor, and Talbot; as you might expect, Peach County is where this drive begins.

We start this visit to west-central Georgia where GA 49 crosses Interstate 75. Taking GA 49 south, you are in the small town of Byron on a four-lane road. There are a number of small restaurants and large gas sta-

Peach orchards in bloom near Fort Valley.

tions that must be passed before you see the first peach orchards. Just out of Byron, the road becomes a divided highway called Peach Parkway. This is rural countryside with a diverse agriculture. A Christmas tree farm is on the right, and pecan groves are frequent on either side of the road. Although you cannot see them from the road, kiwi fruit orchards are advertised and this exotic fruit is grown here.

As soon as you leave I-75, you are only a few miles from the first peach orchards. In early spring the well-groomed, small trees are in perfectly even rows. The pink blooms are a blaze of color blanketing the level to gently rolling countryside. Most of the peach orchards are off the main highway; however, there are enough so that you will see a number of orchards on GA 49.

Peach blossom time is from mid-March to early April, depending on the weather. The vagaries of weather makes peaches a very fickle crop. Blooming season is not very long and can be easily missed. However, there are so many other flowering native trees, shrubs, and vines along the route that if you miss the mass pink of the peach orchards, you still have plenty of other flowers to see. For example, March is also the blooming time for the yellow jasmine, a vine growing up trees along the road; redbud, a small, leguminous tree; wild plums, with masses of white blossoms; and the bright red-winged fruits of the red maple, which add much color to this drive.

From Byron to Fort Valley is 10 miles. As you come into Fort Valley, the Blue Bird Body Company is on either side of the road. This is where most of the yellow school buses you rode as a child are made. The Blue Bird chassis also supports campers and other people-carrying vehicles. Cross over US 341 and continue on GA 49.

Leaving Fort Valley, peach orchards and pecan groves are very evident on both sides of the highway, and in about 14 miles you come to the brick gateway leading to Massee Lane Gardens, home of the American Camellia Society. The attractive Fetterman Building that houses the gift shop, the outstanding collection of porcelain sculptures, and an auditorium with a slide program featuring camellia growing make this well worth the stop. The walk-through gardens have displays of camellias, roses, narcissi, daylilies, chrysanthemums, azaleas, flowering trees, and many other plants blooming in season, along with a quaint Japanese garden. Flowering seasons are: camellias, November–March; narcissi, February–March; azaleas, dogwood, iris and viburnum, March–April; roses, April–November. Wheelchairs are available from which most everything in the gardens can be seen and smelled. This site is surrounded by peach orchards and pecan groves.

Three miles farther, you come to the small town of Marshallville. GA 49 going through this town is lined with camellias, and as you leave the residential area the road is lined with very large crepe myrtle bushes. The camellias bloom through the winter and early spring, and the crepe myrtles bloom during the summer.

Montezuma is the next small town, reached in about 10 miles. This community suffered dramatically from the devastating flood of 1994. A recorded 21 inches of rain fell in a short time in the Flint River watershed. Although the town has made a remarkable recovery from the flood, the effects will be visible for many years to come. GA 49 crosses the Flint River here and through the Oglethorpe community where the large Weyerhauser plant is located.

In another 8 miles, you come to the Andersonville National Historic Site. This unique National Park Service site is the only park to serve as a memorial to all Americans ever held as prisoners of war. It is the site of the Andersonville National Cemetery, which was established in 1865. The initial interments were those 12,914 men who had died in the nearby prison camp. The ultimate tragedy of the Civil War is embodied here at Andersonville. Nearby is the Andersonville Civil War Village. Andersonville hosts the Andersonville Historic Fair the first week in October, when craftsmen such as blacksmiths, potters, and glass blowers demonstrate these and many other early American skills.

It is 9 miles from Andersonville to Americus, the next city on the route. Americus boasts a number of "firsts." Charles Lindbergh bought his first plane and made his first solo flight from Souther Field. This was the first city in Georgia to operate electric street cars. The Brickyard Plantation Golf

The Andersonville National Cemetery was established in 1865.

Club with a beautiful 27-hole golf course and the Lindbergh Memorial are on GA 49. Many attractive old homes are beautifully landscaped with flowering shrubs, including grand arrays of azaleas, dogwoods, and redbuds in spring, and many others blooming throughout the year.

One mile outside Americus, leave GA 49 and continue on U.S. Highway 280 West for 10 miles. This takes you to Plains, the home of thirtyninth U.S. President Jimmy Carter. On the way, you pass through expansive fields of peanuts and other crops, the Southwest Georgia Agricultural Experiment Station, and the Plains Welcome Center. Plains is a small rural town that has remained so even with all the attention that has come to it as the home of a United States President. The drive ends here where you can take a tour of the Jimmy Carter National Historic Site and see other features of this peaceful small agricultural community.

25

Hawkinsville to Lumber City

General description: This drive follows the Ocmulgee River to Lumber City before it joins the Oconee River to become the largest river in the state, the Altamaha River. Cotton, corn, tobacco, and other crops grow in broad fields. The forests are mainly pine plantations grown for pulpwood and timber on the uplands, and hardwoods along the bottomlai.ds of rivers and creeks. The world's record largemouth bass was caught at Montgomery Lake, an oxbow lake beside the Ocmulgee River. A histc ical marker describing the feat is about 5 miles from Jacksonville near the entrance to Horse Creek Wildlife Management Area. Except at bridges, the river is difficult to see because most of the floodplain is a wide, forested swamp.

Special attractions: The drive passes through the upper Coastal Plain. You can see pecan groves, row crops and pastures, many farm ponds, and river swamps. The road crosses the Ocmulgee River at several places. The Double Q kiwi fruit farm is on Georgia Highway 26. The Hawkinsville Harness Horse Training Facility is on U.S. Highway 129 and Georgia Highway 11. Hunting in season, birding, and wildlife watching on Horse Creek Wildlife Management Area and, with permission, on some private lands. Because of the wide range of natural habitats along this drive, it is a fine birding and wildlife watching drive. Side roads, both unpaved and paved, lead to interesting river swampland and help break up the long, straight Georgia Highway 117.

Location: Middle Georgia along the Ocmulgee River.

Drive route numbers: Interstate 75 at Exit 41; Georgia Highway 26; Georgia Highway 11/U.S. Highway 129; Georgia Highway 30/U.S. Highway 280; and Georgia Highway 1'7.

Travel season: Spring is the best time for fishing and flowering trees and shrubs. October and November are best for leaf color and seeing fields of cotton ready for picking. Summer is best for agriculture and the floral displays around homes. Winter weather is mild and there is much to see at this time of the year also.

Camping: Little Ocmulgee State Park with tent, trailer, and RV campsites is at McRae, about 25 miles from Lumber City. Georgia Veterans State Park near Cordele and General Coffee State Park near Douglas also offer year-round camping.

Services: Motels, restaurants, and gas at Exit 41 on I-75 and in Hawkinsville, Lumber City, and Hazlehurst.

Nearby attractions: Little Ocmulgee State Park and its fishing, golfing, and hiking; west of I-75 at Exit 41, near Montezuma, is Yoder's Deitsch

Haus restaurant, famous for its Mennonite food; and Big Hammock Natural Area, about 35 miles from Hazlehurst.

The drive

This drive parallels the course of the Ocmulgee River as it swings in a large arc through central Georgia. It follows an ancient trading path that followed the Altamaha and Ocmulgee rivers from Darien to Fort Hawkins at the present site of Macon. This old river road runs through some of the best hunting and fishing land in the state. Six public Wildlife Management Areas lie either directly on this route or easily accessible from it, and offer hiking, camping, birding, and fishing in addition to hunting opportunities. Private hunting reserves provide guides for game species including white-tailed deer, wild turkey, dove, quail, rabbit, squirrel, and wild hog during state seasons from early fall to late spring. The Ocmulgee itself is a prime fishing stream, offering bluegill, redbreast, crappie, striped bass, catfish, and in particular, largemouth bass. It was in a small oxbow pond off the Ocmulgee that the current world record was caught, a 22-pound, 4-ounce whopper! There is access to the river at more than ten developed landings all the way from Hawkinsville to Lumber City. In addition, Dodge County Public Fishing Area is a 125-acre lake with boat ramps, docks, nature trails, and picnic facilities.

For people whose idea of the sporting life has to do with fine blooded horses, Hawkinsville is the winter training center for standardbred pacers and trotters. Trainers and horse breeders keep their charges fit for the spring and summer harness racing season by exercising them on Hawkinsville's track. Each April, the horses show their stuff at the annual Harness Racing Festival. Just as Hawkinsville enjoys the elegance of sleek standardbreds and sulky drivers in racing silks, Abbeville, 24 miles away, prides itself in matters porcine as the Wild Hog Capital of Georgia; each May, it hosts the Ocmulgee Wild Hog Festival.

Although the route chosen for this drive follows the river's southward loop, you have the option to simply follow U.S. Highway 341 in a straight line from Hawkinsville, through Eastman and McRae, to Lumber City and Hazlehurst. These larger towns have more services; antique seekers and flea-market fanatics can explore shops in each of them.

Interstate access to this drive from I-75 is via GA 26, 18 miles to Hawkinsville. This access is scenic in itself and offers several interesting features, including Double Q Farms, Georgia's largest producer of kiwi fruit. Here you can buy fresh fruit as well as a variety of jellies and jams containing kiwis.

Drive 25: Hawkinsville to Lumber City

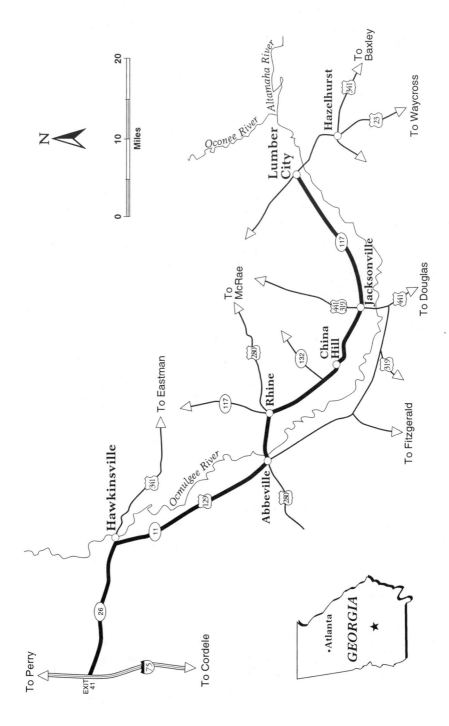

Closer to Hawkinsville on the right is a giant air surveillance antenna operated by the U.S. Navy. Stretching across a flat field all the way to the horizon, this is one of twelve such facilities forming a line across the U.S. at the same latitude (about 32 degrees north) to monitor orbiting objects above earth.

The drive starts in Hawkinsville at the intersection of GA 26 and US 129/341, following US 129 south for the first part of our drive. This leads through town. There are many well-kept homes along this way. A self-guided driving tour is available, along with other information, at the Hawkinsville Chamber of Commerce, which is housed in the Opera House on your left at Lumpkin Street. Beside the Opera House sits "Katie," a steam pumper fire engine built in 1883. It is one of the few of its kind left in the world.

Past the Opera House, follow US 129 as it turns right. Hawkinsville has for years been a place where harness horse trainers come for winter training. On your left, soon after you turn, are the wooden grandstands of the old race track, which operated from the early 1920s to 1976. It has been replaced by the facility you will reach shortly.

On your right, 1 mile past the old track, is the Hawkinsville Training Facility. You can see stables where the horses are kept, and soon you arrive at the actual 1.5-mile race tracks. If your visit is during the winter months, you are likely to see animals being exercised. Visitors are welcome. During the warm months, these standardbred trotters and pacers travel the harness-racing circuit in the North and Midwest. The Harness Racing Festival is held in April as an opportunity for the horses to experience competition before they get out on the racing circuit. As of this writing, Georgia has not legalized parimutuel betting, so you cannot actually place monetary wagers on the races during the festival. It is all for "funsies" unless the law is changed.

Beyond the harness tracks you will come to Gooseneck Farms and The Nuthouse in the Grove, where you will find pecans and pecan candies from locally grown nuts, as well as gift items. The land opens into broad fields, and in the warm months, the sandy soil is planted in cotton, soybeans, and peanuts. One indicator of the importance of agriculture is that farm homes are often dwarfed by the equipment sheds and barns surrounding them. Some of the fields are irrigated by pumping groundwater up through huge sprinklers that travel on wheels in arcs a quarter mile to the center.

Much of the land is also devoted to another crop: trees. You will pass orchards with orderly rows of stately pecan trees, and will also very likely see trucks hauling pine and hardwood logs to paper factories and sawmills. More than half the land here is timberland, and has been for years. In fact, Dodge County is named for William E. Dodge, a New York lumberman who had large holdings in this area.

Streams such as Big Tuckasawhatchee Creek are typical of South Georgia; slow-moving and meandering, their banks are shaded by yellow poplar, oak, sycamore, and sweetgum trees, the branches festooned with Spanish moss.

Abbeville, home each May of the Ocmulgee Wild Hog Festival is 20 miles south of Hawkinsville. Turn left onto US 280. The Wilcox County Courthouse, an elaborate brick building built in 1903, is on the left as you make your turn.

Heading out of town on US 280, you travel a raised roadway built across the floodplain of the Ocmulgee River. The Ocmulgee begins near Jackson, flows across the Fall Line at Macon, passes the Ocmulgee Mounds, and then makes a big arc to the southeast, finally joining the Oconee River near Lumber City to form the Altamaha.

There are wide, water-filled ditches on either side of the road. These are borrow-pits, where highway builders "borrowed" the dirt used to raise the road out of flood's way above the river-bottom swamp.

On the far side of the river, you enter Rhine. Turn right on GA 117; you will follow this highway for the remainder of the drive. This road parallels the east bank of the river. As we mentioned before, expect to see logging trucks, particularly on this road. It is 20 miles to Jacksonville. This drive is along the dividing line between the upper and lower Coastal Plain, which

The Ocmulgee River near Jacksonville has
extensive bottomland hardwood swamps on both sides.

Historical marker for world record largemouth bass caught near here in Montgomery Lake, an overflow oxbow of the Ocmulgee River.

was caused by rising and falling of sea levels that alternately covered and exposed this land during the Cretaceous period less than 130 million years ago. On the right, past China Hill, is the 5,800-acre Muskhogean Wildlife Management Area. The name is one of the several used to describe the Indian tribes in central and southern Georgia. The more common title for these people is Creek. This is the smaller of two WMAs located directly along GA 117.

At the intersection of GA 117 with US 441/319, is the village of Jacksonville. Once an important city along the River Road, Jacksonville Landing on the Ocmulgee was a shipping point for passengers and freight for the nearby plantations. Now it is little more than a crossroads. Almost immediately past Jacksonville, you enter Horse Creek Wildlife Management Area. Administered by the Georgia Department of Natural Resources, this 8,500-acre facility provides public hunting and fishing as well as hiking, birding, and boat and canoe access to the Ocmulgee River.

About 4 miles past Jacksonville, at a clearing in the pine forest on the left, is Georgia's only historic marker about a fish. On June 2, 1932, at Montgomery Lake, an oxbow lake on the Ocmulgee near here, nineteen-year-old George Perry landed the biggest largemouth black bass ever caught, a 22-pound, 4-ounce superlunker. This world record has not been bettered as of this writing, more than sixty years later. Considering the popularity of bass fishing, it is surprising there is no more shrine to the event than this historic marker, which may be obscured by roadside vegetation.

Fifteen miles later, you enter Lumber City. As you may gather from the name, this was a center of timber production. Logs and finished lumber were shipped down the Altamaha River from here to the coast at Darien. GA 117 ends at the intersection with US 341/23. You may go 24 miles northwest to reach McRae, or 7 miles southeast to visit Hazlehurst.

26

McRae to Reidsville

General description: From McRae to Vidalia, Lyons, and Reidsville, you are in the Coastal Plain. After you cross the lower end of Oconee River, large farms and pecan groves are broken only by areas of forest, where it is too wet to farm. The core drive totals about 55 miles, with side trips possibly adding another 30 miles.

Special attractions: Little Ocmulgee State Park; the famous Vidalia onion farms; Gordonia Alatamaha State Park; Plant Hatch nuclear power site; and Big Hammock Natural Area. State parks have interesting hiking trails.

Location: Southeast Georgia, just south of Interstate 16.

Drive route numbers: U.S. Highways 280 and 1, and Georgia Highway 121.

Travel season: An all-season drive. However, biting gnats and mosquitoes are least bothersome during the cooler months.

Camping: Little Ocmulgee State Park and Lodge and Gordonia Alatamaha State Park have tent and trailer camping.

Services: Lodging and food are available in the larger towns, especially McRae, Vidalia, and Reidsville.

Nearby attractions: Lumber City, Ocmulgee River, Altamaha River, and the site of the world-record largemouth bass near Jacksonville, and Georgia Veterans and General Coffee state parks.

 The drive

This is a short drive along US 280, with several interesting possible side trips. US 280 goes from Birmingham, Alabama, to Savannah, Georgia. This segment in central Georgia is wholly in the drainage basin of the Altamaha River, the largest undammed river in the Southeast. The highway crosses the Oconee River which, with the Ocmulgee, is a major tributary to the Altamaha. In addition, it crosses the Little Ocmulgee River, Alligator Creek, and the Ohoopee River. This is largely agricultural land, producing corn, cotton, peanuts, soybeans, pecans, and, most notably, Vidalia sweet onions.

Side trips at either end of the drive can satisfy a sweet tooth. At Eastman, Stuckey Candies is famous for its pecan rolls and other confections, and Claxton is home to Claxton Fruitcake, known nationwide. The Claxton Fruitcake Company bakes over a million pounds of cake a year and tours

Drive 26: McRae to Reidsville

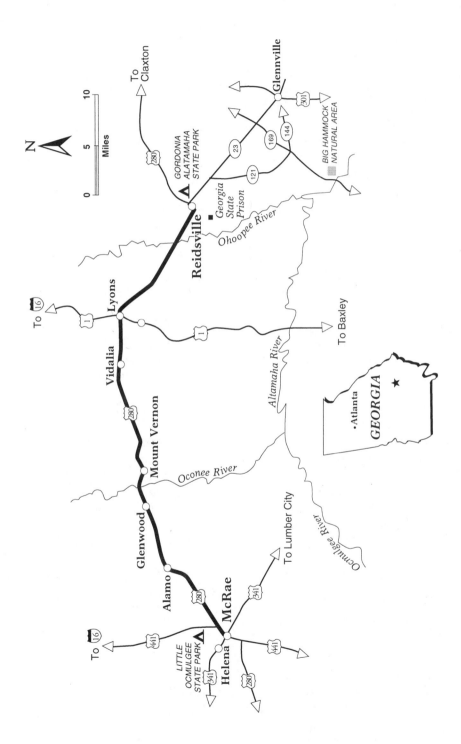

(and tastes) are available. Claxton also is home to the honey sweetness of Wilbanks Apiary, a major beekeeping operation. Not as sweet, but with a bite of its own, is Claxton's annual rattlesnake roundup the second weekend in March.

South of Vidalia on U.S. Highway 1 near the Altamaha River is Plant Hatch, a nuclear power generating facility. Animated exhibits at the Edwin I. Hatch Visitor Center explain the use of atomic energy.

Also near the Altamaha are Bullard Creek Wildlife Management Area (WMA), off U.S. Highway 221 between Uvalda and Hazlehurst, and Big Hammock WMA, on US 144 south of Reidsville and Glennville. These sites offer exceptional hunting and fishing, as well as hiking, boating, and birding.

Interstate 16 is north of our route and runs roughly parallel to it. Access is available to and from I-16 at all towns on the drive.

The drive begins in McRae at the intersection of U.S. Highways 280, 23, 441/319, and 341. This intersection is called Liberty Square. The reason is obvious: a homegrown Statue of Liberty lifting her torch in a small park. It was erected by the local Lions Club. You cannot miss it, nor should you. Go east on US 280. Just north of McRae, US 441 splits to go north. A half mile up US 441 is the entrance to Little Ocmulgee State Park. During the Great Depression, local people wanted a place to swim, camp, and fish, so they donated land along the Little Ocmulgee River. The National Park Service and Civilian Conservation Corps built a park, and it opened in 1940. There is a 265-acre lake and an eighteen-hole golf course, as well as picnicking, campsites, and cottages.

You know you have reached the Coastal Plain. The soil is sandy, and the Little Ocmulgee River and Alligator Creek are slow-flowing, tannic-acid-stained streams the color of strong tea. US 280 runs straight, as if it were surveyed with a rifle. The road gently undulates along the former seabed for 5 miles before it finally reaches the first curve. Agriculture is the main business here. You will see stands of loblolly and longleaf pine trees; cotton fields; signs advertising seed suppliers, farm equipment companies, and promoting local pork producers; and a sign erected by the local chapter of Future Farmers of America marking their experimental forest several miles from McRae.

It is about 16 miles to Alamo. The town's business district runs on either side of a railroad track that parallels the highway, and through town, there are about 200 yards of open space bordering the tracks where trucks from the fields can park to unload their crops into the grain elevators located there.

A couple of miles east of Alamo you pass a fire tower on the left at the Georgia Forestry Commission office. Towers such as this one were once located widely over the state. People sat in these towers and scanned the countryside to spot telltale wisps of smoke rising from forest fires in order

Longleaf pines festooned with Spanish moss at
Little Ocmulgee State Park near McRae.

to spread the alarm. Some are still in use, but most have been closed.

Three miles past the fire tower, go through Glenwood and continue across the Oconee River. This large river springs from headwaters in the Piedmont near Athens, over 160 miles away. Unlike the languid darkwater streams you have so far encountered, the Oconee is much larger, lighter in color, and brisker in flow. Soon you enter Mount Vernon, a town of pleasant, one-story, ranch-style brick houses, with Saint Augustine grass lawns under the shade of tall longleaf pines. There are a number of well-maintained turn-of-the-century frame homes as well. As Mount Vernon merges into Ailey, you will see the campus of Brewton-Parker College on the left. This is a two-year college affiliated with the Baptist church. It has an enrollment of around 1,300 students. This is simple, unpretentious country where road-side parks offer picnic tables in the shade of the pines every few miles. It is the kind of country where people still practice civility toward each other.

There are of groves of pecan trees on either side of the road. These orchards of tall, well-formed trees in orderly rows look like manicured parks. Georgia is the largest pecan-producing state in America, but the thing that this particular section is noted for grows closer to the ground. This is the home of the famous Vidalia sweet onion. In 1931, a farmer named Mose Coleman grew a crop of onions that were exceptionally sweet. Since then, the onions from this area have become renowned for their mild taste and are eagerly sought after by consumers. The onion plants are a variety developed in Texas and are grown other places, but the high sulfur content in the soil of the Georgia Coastal Plain is claimed to be the element that makes Vidalia onions stand above the rest. The onion region covers several counties, but all call their produce Vidalia onions.

In the fall and early winter, workers in vast fields place each onion set by hand. A half-year later, the succulent bulbs are harvested in April, May, and June. Vidalia holds a ten-day-long Onion Festival in late April and early May. You can contact the Vidalia Welcome Center to find out the exact dates and to arrange tours of the local farms and packing sheds (see the appendix). In August and September, tours are available of cotton and tobacco fields. In these late summer months you can smell the cured tobacco in warehouses that border US 280 in Vidalia. You may visit the warehouses, where the song of the auctioneer sets the price the farmer will get. Buyers travel to the region's warehouses in a circuit, so the scheduling of sale days varies through the season, which lasts from mid-July to mid-October. To find what days sales will be held, you may inquire of warehouse people or contact the Vidalia Welcome Center.

A less-known attraction of Vidalia is the Ladson Genealogical Library. It is a center of genealogical research, with one of the largest libraries in the Southeast. The collection available to people searching for their family records includes books, pamphlets, and microfilm.

It is obvious by the size and activity in town that Vidalia has been well-treated by agriculture. The road here becomes multi-laned, and as it goes through town, shopping centers line the roadsides. This four-lane highway continues to Lyons, 6 miles away. As you drive, you will pass a number of outlets selling Vidalia onions, some of them at storage facilities. At one time, the onions were available only for a month or so around harvest time, but now storage facilities have been developed to keep the onions fresh-tasting for months, so they are available practically year-round.

Although Vidalia is the better-known town in Toombs County, Lyons is the county seat. The county is named for Robert Toombs, secretary of state of the Confederacy. Robert Toombs Inn is a local bed and breakfast. Toombs himself lived in Washington, Georgia (See Drive 16).

For a side trip, a journey 17 miles south of Lyons on US 1 takes you to Plant Hatch nuclear power facility. The plant is located near where US 1 crosses the Altamaha River. The Edwin I. Hatch Nuclear Plant Visitor Center offers animated exhibits that explain how atomic power is used to generate electricity.

Ten miles past Lyons on US 280, you cross the Ohoopee River, a beautiful south Georgia blackwater stream running over white sand and shaded by blackgum, willow, water oak and sweet bay. The Ohoopee River Plantation on Georgia Highway 56 offers canoe trips, picnicking, and fishing on the river.

Reidsville, 7 miles past the Ohoopee, is the location of the Georgia state prison. It is also the location of Gordonia Alatamaha State Park. The park is inside the town, to the left down a shaded drive past the playing fields of Reidsville High School. It is a relatively small facility, only 280 acres, but offers swimming, picnicking, miniature golf, camping, lake fishing, and a nine-hole golf course, which is watered and nourished by treated wastewater. This land application treatment keeps from releasing the sewer water into any local streams, and it has no odor or unpleasant effect on the golf course.

Gordonia Alatamaha Park is named for a flowering plant discovered nearby by botanist William Bartram on one of his travels through Georgia in the 1700s. Bartram collected a specimen of the plant, returned with it to his home in Philadelphia, and rooted it. Descendants of that plant are still available in nurseries. Oddly, the plant Bartram found and named has never been seen in the wild since.

The thing that Reidsville is most famous for is the Georgia State Prison, located just south of town on GA 147. Many Reidsville residents work at the prison, and inmate labor has been used to build the structures at the State Park. It is ironic that this drive begins with the embodiment of freedom at McRae's Liberty Square, and ends with the embodiment of confinement at the prison.

You may continue on US 280, 13 miles to Claxton, the fruitcake capital and home of the Rattlesnake Roundup, or follow GA 23 for 14 miles to Glennville. Besides onions and vegetables at the State Farmers Market, Glennville offers the nearby Big Hammock Natural Area, a large sand ridge bordering the Altamaha River within the Big Hammock Wildlife Management Area, and Phillips Natural Area, an 800-acre nature preserve.

Drive 27: Valdosta to Thomasville

Lakeland, Hahira, Barney, Pavo

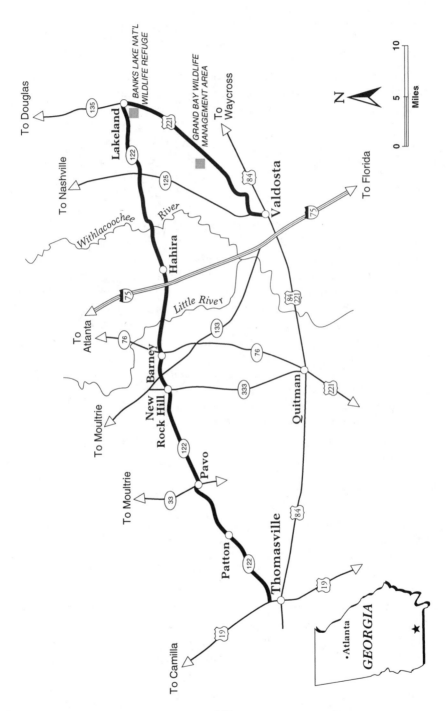

27

Valdosta to Thomasville

Lakeland, Hahira, Barney, Pavo

General description: This drive of about 95 miles has something for everyone. It leads along the southern part of the Coastal Plain, and from Valdosta to Banks Lake and Hahira, the land is flat with large fields of row crops. Except for the cities at the beginning and end, the drive features farm country. From Hahira to Thomasville the topography becomes more gently rolling. Peach orchards, pecan groves, peanut, tobacco, and corn fields, and mature forests add to the pastoral nature of this drive. The birder and wildlife watcher will find plenty of variety along the country roads.

Special attractions: Grand Bay Wildlife Management Area and its boardwalk, observation tower, and environmental education center; Banks Lake, a picturesque, cypress-studded, dark-water lake; peach orchards, pecan groves, and blueberry farming; Hahira, a center of the state honey industry; and Thomasville, the "City of Roses."

Location: South Georgia, very near the Florida-Georgia state line. Valdosta is at Exit 4 on Interstate 75.

Drive route numbers: Interstate 75, U.S. Highway 221/84, Georgia Highway 31/ U.S. Highway 221, and Georgia Highway 122.

Travel season: A year-round drive. June is the best month for most of the fruit orchards. Winter is great for migratory birds in the Grand Bay Wildlife Management Area and Banks Lake National Wildlife Refuge. Flowering trees and shrubs are at their peak in early spring. Fall leaf color usually peaks in late October and November.

Camping: Nearest opportunities are at Reed Bingham State Park north of Hahira and General Coffee State Park near Douglas.

Services: Valdosta and Thomasville have many motels and restaurants. Gas is available throughout the drive.

Nearby attractions: Moody Air Force Base; Reed Bingham State Park, its many wintering vultures and annual "Buzzard Day" festival; camping, fishing, and butterfly and hummingbird gardens; canoeing on the peaceful, black-water Alapaha, Withlacoochee, and Ochlockonee rivers; the Georgia Agrirama at Tifton and its nineteenth-century living history museum with restored farm buildings, rural town, and gift shop.

The drive

This drive is shaped like a "J" lying on its side. The curved part of the "J" is a swing from Valdosta, past Grand Bay Wildlife Management Area to Lakeland, and back north of Banks Lake National Wildlife Refuge. Within this arc is Moody Air Force Base, and a large wetland that drains into the Alapaha River and Grand Bay Creek.

Past Grand Bay WMA, the route heads west through Hahira, Barney, and Pavo, and finishes at Thomasville, "The Rose City." In essence, you travel from swamp to sophistication. Grand Bay and Banks Lake lure sportsmen with their wealth of waterfowl, hogs, and deer and with the excellent fishing in their waters. Outdoor lovers enjoy beautiful swamp scenery, and wildlife ranging from alligators to ospreys and eagles. At the other end of the drive, Thomasville has long been an overwintering spot for the wealthy. Following the Civil War, industrial moguls bought plantations in south Georgia as private hunting preserves where they could enjoy mild winters and shoot quail over keen-nosed hunting dogs. Many of these plantations still operate today, and Thomasville boasts many fine homes as well as its famous rose gardens.

The middle of the trip goes through fertile Coastal Plain fields planted in cotton, tobacco, vegetables, peaches, and blueberries, and through the charmingly named towns of Barney, Hahira, and Pavo—an added bonus, with Valdosta, for people who like to boast of the places they've been. The route touches Interstate 75 at Valdosta and Hahira. The most comfortable time to take this trip is during the fall, winter, and spring. Summers in south Georgia can be scorchingly hot and humid, but visits this time of year let you stop at roadside stands to stock up on fruit and produce from farms along the way. Drive 28, Okefenokee Swamp Loop, and Drive 23, Bainbridge to Eufaula, are near this drive.

The drive begins in Valdosta, heading north on U.S. Highway 221 at its intersection with U.S. Highway 84. The late humorist H. Allen Smith claimed that every joke and funny story in the world originated in Valdosta. This may be an exaggeration, but it is no joke that Valdosta is best known for its high school football teams. The Valdosta High Wildcats are legendary for being a perennial national powerhouse in schoolboy sport. There are plans to open a national high school football hall of fame here. The city grew from the riches of the land. It was an early center for Sea Island cotton, as well as hub of products gleaned from the pine forests including lumber and naval stores, products such as pitch, pine tar, and turpentine made from pine rosin. The historical society museum in the old Carnegie Library on Central Avenue (US 84) has a display from those days. There are three districts in town on the National Register of Historic Places and several fine

Peach picking near Pavo.

homes, particularly on North Patterson Street (Georgia Highway 7 Alternate). Valdosta–Lowndes County Convention and Visitors Bureau offers a self-guided driving tour.

Continue following US 221 as it bears left toward Lakeland. The road soon leaves Valdosta behind and runs dead straight, undulating gently across the Coastal Plain through oak and pine forest and along fields.

Eight miles out of town near mile marker 25 on US 221, Knights Academy Road leads left 1.5 miles to the entrance of Grand Bay Wildlife Management Area. These 9,400 acres of lowland swamp are administered by the Georgia Department of Natural Resources for public hunting and fishing and as a nature education center. For students and visitors, a boardwalk leads to a tower with a panoramic view above the cypress trees and flooded plain. Besides the natural beauty, you can often see planes taking off from Moody Air Force Base. The U. S. Air Force uses part of the wetland as a bombing range, and it is not unusual to have your contemplation of nature interrupted by low-flying jets roaring overhead. This does not seem to bother the ducks and alligators living here very much at all.

Continuing on US 221, you will pass the Grand Bay WMA checkstation on the left. This is headquarters for deer, small game, and waterfowl hunts in season. You will cross Grand Bay Creek, one of the streams fed by the wetland, and in 2 miles on your right, is an enormous lawn. It is a sod field. They grow Bermuda grass here, cut up the sod, and ship it to landscapers who plant the squares to create instant lawns. There are several of these sod fields on either side of the road before you reach Lakeland, a nice town with neat, attractive bungalows set in pine-shaded yards.

Here you turn left onto GA 122. Note: You are turning off US 221 onto GA 122. It can be confusing if you stumble over numbers. You will soon see Banks Lake on your left; there is a small parking lot here. This National Wildlife Refuge is also one of the largest natural lakes in Georgia. Most of the state's lakes are backed up behind manmade dams; Banks Lake is there because nature put it there. It is a large example of a Carolina Bay, a roughly circular depression common in the Coastal Plain north into the Carolinas. Grand Bay is another example. Some claim these are the result of meteorites striking Earth. No one knows for sure what their origin is. On a calm day, the lake is like a mirror reflecting the surrounding cypress trees and clouds overhead. Occasionally an alligator will cruise by, or a fish will splash, disturbing the calm surface. Fishing is excellent here, but at this writing no boat rentals are available, so you must make your own arrangements to actually cruise these dark waters. You may, however, enjoy the scenery from a small walkway built out into the lake some 100 feet.

Beyond the parking area, there are several private cabins built on the shores, and soon you can no longer see the lake, even though the highway is

Banks Lake National Wildlife Refuge near Lakeland.

gently curving around its north end. The roadside land is swampy, with Spanish moss festooning the live oak trees.

Seven miles from Lakeland, GA 125 leads 3 miles to the left, to Moody Air Force Base, home of the 347th Wing of the Air Combat Command. Our route keeps us on GA 122, where the swampy scenery is replaced by pastures and fields of tobacco or soybeans. In south Georgia, farmers till the high ground and leave the stream bottoms pretty well alone. In north Georgia, which is mountainous, the desirable farms are in the bottomland, with the upland left to forest.

In the fields, you are likely to see large, white birds with long legs and long necks and beaks. These are cattle egrets. Native to Africa, they evidently were storm-blown across the Atlantic Ocean to South America in this century, and have spread to the fields and pastures of North America.

On the right is the entrance gate to Georgia Sheriffs Boys Ranch, a home for underprivileged and neglected youngsters operated by the Georgia Sheriffs Association.

Three and a half miles after you cross the Withlacoochee River, you enter Hahira (pronounced "hay-HI-ra"). Each October, Hahira hosts a Honeybee Festival honoring the town's position as a center of honey production. Bees from South Georgia are well-traveled. Growers load flatbed trucks with hundreds of hives in the spring and drive them as far away as North Dakota, where the bees earn their keep producing clover honey all summer. In the fall, the hives return to Georgia where these industrious insects make their golden sweetness all winter.

Stay on GA 122 through the heart of Hahira across Interstate 75 about 7 miles to Barney. There are peach orchards on either side of the road. If your trip is in the months from late spring to late September, you may plan a stop at one of the packing houses here. They offer orchard-fresh peaches, blueberries, melons straight from the fields, as well as prepared jams and jellies.

This area is seriously agricultural. Local farms grow tomatoes, peppers, tobacco, peanuts, cotton, and bedding plants. Many of the seedlings you purchase at your local garden center were sprouted in the sandy South Georgia soil.

Beyond Barney, GA 122 leads 15 miles to Pavo (pronounced "PAY-vo"). First Valdosta, then Hahira, now Pavo. Think how envious your friends will be when you tell them where you've been. Pavo, incidentally, is Latin for "peacock." If you are hungry when you get here, you will have to ask where to eat; the local restaurant has no sign, but the food there is tasty.

GA 122 leads 15 miles to Thomasville, the City of Roses. Thomasville boasts more rose plants (20,000) than people (19,000). Roses decorate the city's police cars. The town became a wintering spot for the wealthy in the 1880s when the mild climate drew visitors, as did the supposed benefits of breathing pine-scented air. A number of elaborate Victorian mansions and quail-hunting plantations attest to the city's popularity. Lapham-Patterson House is a State Historic Site, with hourly tours of this 1885 "cottage" built by a Chicago shoe merchant. Pebble Hill Plantation is a turn-of-the-century shooting preserve.

Thomasville's welcome center on South Broad Street has a self-guided driving tour. To reach the welcome center, continue straight where GA 122 becomes Remington Avenue, into downtown Thomasville, and turn right on South Broad St.

28

Okefenokee Swamp Loop

Waycross, Folkston, Fargo, Homerville

General description: This 150-mile loop drive completely circles the Okefenokee Swamp. An additional 65 miles are added when you drive in and out of the three access roads to the swamp proper. The swamp is almost completely in the 438,000-acre Okefenokee National Wildlife Refuge and Wilderness Area. The largest and most ecologically intact swamp in America, it is easily accessed at three points along the drive route. The highways around the swamp are, for the most part, very level and straight. This drive then passes through large tracts of coastal pine plantations and some mixed hardwood and pine forests owned by large timber companies. It is possible to travel many miles and yet see few homes from the roadways. You can drive to the swamp's edge at Suwannee Canal Recreation Area, Stephen C. Foster State Park, or Okefenokee Swamp Park. Visitor centers, educational displays, boardwalks into the swamp, canoe and boat rental, hiking trails, observation towers, and many other activities are available at these points.

Special attractions: Okefenokee Swamp is the main attraction. Wildlife viewing offers a wide variety of species, including deer, raccoon, fox squirrels, armadillos, many large wading birds, birds of prey, snakes, and even the rare black bear. Birders may find the red-cockaded woodpecker along the Swamp Island Drive at the Suwannee Canal Recreation Area. The boardwalk from Chesser Island into the swamp ends at a 50-foot viewing tower. Boating and canoeing is available at both the east and west entrance. Fishing, birding, wildlife watching, boating and canoeing, hiking, and bicycling are among the many activities available at Suwannee Canal Recreation Area and Stephen C. Foster State Park.

Location: Extreme southeastern corner of Georgia.

Drive route numbers: U.S. Highways 1/23, 84, and 441; Georgia Highways 121, 23, 94, and 177; and Florida Highway 2.

Travel season: A year-round drive. Many migratory birds use the swamp during spring and fall migrations and many, like sandhill cranes, winter in the swamp. There is also a resident flock of sandhills that nest in the swamp. Alligators are most active during the warmer months, but may even be seen on rare occasions in winter. Spring is best for flowers and nesting birds; fall, for migrating birds and pleasant weather. Biting flies are less of a problem from late fall through the winter and into early spring.

Camping: Stephen C. Foster State Park has well-equipped cabins and

Drive 28: Okefenokee Swamp Loop

Waycross, Folkston, Fargo, Homerville

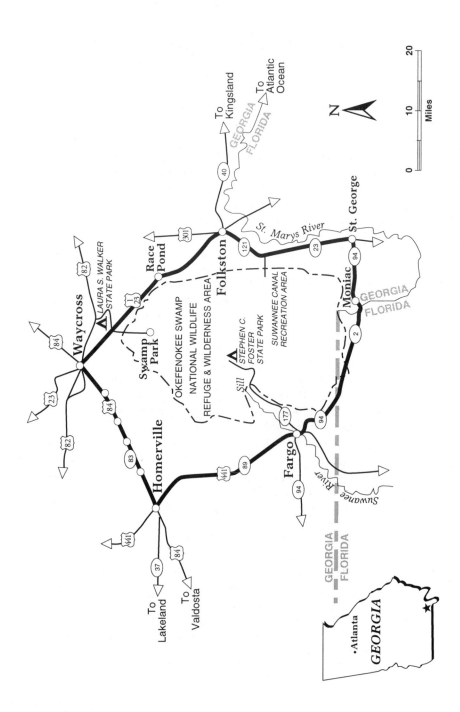

tent, trailer, and RV sites. Tent and trailer camping is available at Laura S. Walker State Park located near Waycross.

Services: Motels and restaurants in Waycross and Folkston. Fargo has a small motel and restaurant. Bed and breakfasts at Homerville. Gas is available at the small towns along the drive.

Nearby attractions: Laura S. Walker State Park, the Atlantic Ocean, and Cumberland Island National Seashore.

 # The drive

This drive begins at Waycross, and makes a complete loop before ending at Waycross again. Within this circle lies south Georgia's Okefenokee Swamp, which is the reason for taking this drive in the first place. Most of the roads along the way are flat and straight, and much of the roadside scenery consists of unrelieved vistas of slash and longleaf pines. These are beautiful trees, but once you have seen the first few thousand of them, they all begin to look alike. Unless you are a devoted fan of pine trees this makes each community you come to a welcome change of scenery, and it makes the spectacular vistas of the swamp even more striking. To see the swamp itself, you must enter at one of the three major access points. This drive will touch all three. Northernmost and easiest to handle for the casual tourist is Okefenokee Swamp Park. Farther south on the eastern side is the U.S. Fish and Wildlife Service's Suwannee Canal Recreation Area, headquarters for the Okefenokee National Wildlife Refuge and Wilderness Area. The third access is Stephen C. Foster State Park on the west of the swamp near Fargo.

The Okefenokee was formed over 250,000 years ago when the ocean covered what is now South Georgia. When sea level dropped, water was trapped behind what had been an underwater ridge. Today the swamp covers nearly a half million acres, of which 438,000 acres are protected as the Okefenokee National Wildlife Refuge. It is a land of great cypress hammocks reflected in the mirror of slow-moving, tannin-stained water, of sandy palmetto and pine islands, and of broad grassy wetland prairies. It is home to the sandhill crane, the heron, the osprey, the prothonotary warbler, and the pileated woodpecker. It is roamed by raccoons, whitetail deer, black bear, otters and wildcats. It is the lair of the endangered eastern indigo snake, and of the eastern diamondback rattlesnake and cottonmouth. It is the domain of the American alligator.

While the swamp is the major attraction, there are other points of interest at Waycross, Folkston, Fargo, and Homerville. The southern portion of the route is in Florida, on a road that may be the only highway in the Sunshine State without a single tourist attraction.

The most comfortable time to visit is during the cool months of late fall, winter, and early spring. Summer heat can be oppressive, especially coupled with the high humidity you can expect here. At any time of year, bring along insect repellent. A variety of biting flies like mosquitoes, no-see-ums, and other bugs are usually waiting to feast on you. However, in winter and very early spring the insects are not bad.

Fishing for warmouth, bluegill, crappie, largemouth bass, bowfin, and chain pickerel is a popular pastime on swamp waters. Hunting is allowed only on a very limited basis on the upland fringe around the 483,000-acre national wildlife refuge.

The nearest interstate highway is I-95, which you can reach from Waycross via U.S. Highway 82, and from Folkston via Georgia Highway 40, the Okefenokee Parkway.

The drive begins in Waycross on U.S. Highway 23 at its intersection with U.S. Highways 84 and 1. Waycross is the first crossing point north of the Okefenokee. U.S. Highways 1, 301, 23, 82, and 84 come together here, as do rail lines from six directions. This was an important route for the Creek Indians and settlers who followed.

Today, Waycross is known as a center for forest products. In addition to logs for pulp and lumber, the pine trees provide rosin which is distilled to make turpentine. Southern Forest World is an industry-sponsored educational exhibit with nature trails and a fire tower. It is next-door to the Okefenokee Heritage Center on North Augusta Avenue (US 301). Recently open is Obediah's Okefenok, a restored 1830 swamper's homestead at the fringe of the Okefenokee on Swamp Road.

The route takes you south, under the railroad, and then alongside the tracks on the left. Also on the left is Memorial Stadium, the community ballpark. It is home to an annual all-night gospel-sing Labor Day weekend. This event draws religious singing groups from a wide area who entertain fans parked in their lawn chairs in front of the stage on the field. The old-time gospel music continues all day and all night. Bear right following US 23/1 south on the four-lane highway. The swamp dictates where the roads go, so these major north-south thoroughfares travel the natural passageway as did the Kings Road, which carried English soldiers to fight the Spanish, and American troops to fight the Seminoles. The road is not as heavily traveled as it was before I-95 and Interstate 75 captured most of the Florida-bound traffic. About 6 miles from Waycross is the entrance road leading 8 miles to Okefenokee Swamp Park. Owned and operated by the city of Waycross and Ware County, it offers boat tours, an interpretive center, and exhibits of swamp life and swamp living.

Along the highway about 6 miles south of the park is the site of Fort Mudge. In the years when the turpentine industry was more active, this was a collection point for the pine rosin harvest. Workers ranged into the piney woods, making chevron cuts in the pine bark and placing cups to catch the dripping sap, much the same way maple trees are tapped in New England. The rosin would be used for caulking ships and barrels or distilled into turpentine. Georgia was once the nation's leading producer of these naval stores. Camps like Fort Mudge no longer operate, and there is no sign here that the place ever existed. We mention Fort Mudge because cartoonist Walt Kelly located his comic strip "Pogo" here. Kelly's characters Pogo Possum, Albert Alligator, Churchy LaFemme the turtle, and Miz Mamzelle Hepzibah the skunk dwelt in the Okefenokee and shopped at Mr. Miggle's Store at the Fort Mudge Memorial Dump. Kelly himself lived in Connecticut, but his characters lived in the Okefenokee.

Race Pond community is 12 miles from the swamp park entrance. The Creek Indians who were here when the first white settlers arrived in Georgia did not take kindly to the newcomers to their land. Bands of the group

The boardwalk at the Okefenokee Swamp in Okefenokee National Wildlife Refuge.

known as the Seminole hid in the swamp and emerged for raids on homesteads and communities until 1838. U.S. Army troops guarding the settlements occupied their off-duty hours racing horses around a pond here. Continue south through Homeland community and on to Folkston. The railroad depot here houses the chamber of commerce and a museum of railroad artifacts.

In Folkston, turn right onto Georgia Highways 23 and 121. About 2 miles from town on Post Road is Sardis Church. Founded around 1821, its pulpit still bears a bullet hole from the Indian wars.

Two miles farther a historic marker describes Traders Hill. A bulwark against Indian attack, it was a trading center and shipping point at the head of navigation of the Saint Marys River.

Four miles later, a right turn onto GA 121 Spur leads 3 miles to Suwannee Canal Recreation Area. The U.S. Fish and Wildlife Service has headquarters here for the Okefenokee National Wildlife Refuge and Wilderness Area, as well as boat rentals and a 7-mile wildlife drive leading past white paint-marked nesting trees of the endangered red-cockaded woodpecker and the Chesser Homestead to a boardwalk that extends almost a mile into the swamp, ending at a 50-foot-high observation tower.

Here on the eastern side of the swamp, boat trails lead into grassy wetland prairies and among tree-covered islands known locally as "houses." Boats and guided tours are available at the refreshment center near the visitor center with many displays of swamp life and history.

Logging operations here cut giant bald cypress trees for their prized rot-resistant lumber until the swamp became a national refuge in 1937. An attempt was made to drain the swamp, and remains of the canal dug for that purpose are still visible near the visitor center and wildlife drive.

Continue on GA 23 past the turnoff to Suwannee Canal through 23 miles of piney woods to Saint George. Turn right onto GA 94, going west across what is known as the Big Bend. This section of Georgia is a peninsula thrust south into Florida. It is caused by the course of the Saint Marys River which rises from the swamp and forms the state line as it flows east to the Atlantic at the town of Saint Marys. It is 12 miles across the Big Bend on GA 94 to the Florida state line at Moniac. Here the road becomes Florida Highway 2 for 15 featureless, dead-straight, pine tree bordered miles until it re-enters Georgia and becomes GA 94 again. Eight miles later, U.S. Highway 441 joins GA 94 and GA 177 turns right, leading to Stephen C. Foster State Park and the Suwannee Sill. It is 12 miles from the turnoff to the sill, a low dam intended to lessen wildfire damage by holding water in the Okefenokee. Research showed that naturally occurring fires burn vegetation that would otherwise sink to the bottom and fill the swamp, so the sill's floodgates are left open to allow nature to work in its own way. Today the sill is used mainly as a boat launch area.

Chesser Prairie in Okefenokee Swamp from the tower at the end of the boardwalk.

Stephen C. Foster State Park, 2 miles past the sill turnoff, is the only developed camping and lodging available in the Okefenokee. You can also rent a boat or canoe or take a pontoon boat tour from here.

The west side of the swamp is the wet side. Waterways range from broad boulevards to narrow, serpentine paths. Anglers come for the very fine warmouth fishing, and birders train their binoculars on ibis, egrets, prothonotary warblers, sandhill cranes, and the rest of the 225 bird species that use the swamp. Everybody can count on seeing numerous alligators cruising the tea-colored, tannin-stained water. Once on the endangered list, alligators have made a spectacular comeback. Stephen C. Foster, for whom the park is named, is composer of the song "Swannee River." This stream flows from the swamp at the Suwannee Sill. Foster, incidentally, never saw the Suwannee River. He used it because it fit the meter of his song. A half mile on GA 94 past the turnoff to Stephen C. Foster Park, a bridge crosses the Suwannee River itself, flowing dark between white sand banks. You may sing if you like. Across the bridge you enter Fargo, where GA 94 turns left. Continue on US 441 for 27 miles to Homerville. Here US 84 leads back to Waycross 27 miles to the east, or to Valdosta 34 miles to the west. Continuing north 36 miles on US 441 will take you to Douglas.

Drive 29: Georgia Coast - Ruins, Marshes, and Rich Folks

Midway to Brunswick

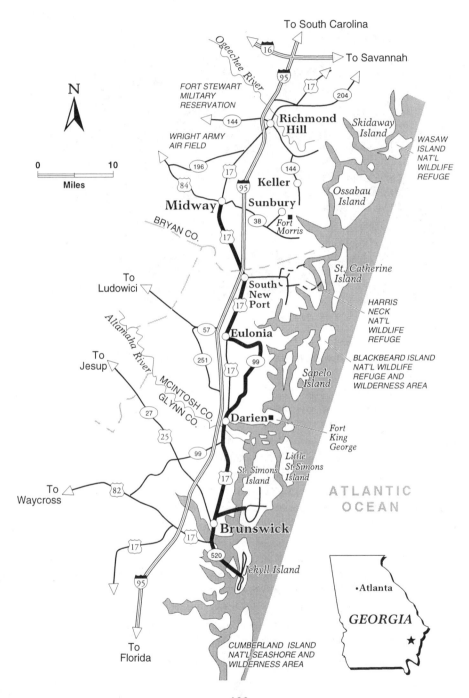

29

Georgia Coast - Ruins, Marshes, and Rich Folks

Midway to Brunswick

General description: As you travel this route of about 65 miles along the colonial coast of Georgia, you will pass through a long history of human activity from that of the earliest American Indians to our society's modern condominiums. This drive follows old U.S. Highway 17. Live oaks, Spanish moss, palmetto and marsh grass, historic plantations and new waterfront cottages, old forts, and a nuclear submarine base characterize this fascinating country.

Special attractions: Many historic landmark areas, including Fort McAllister, Fort King George, and Fort Morris, depict old military operations. The "Liberty Ship" model in Brunswick shows a part of more modern military history. Other features include the preserved Hofwyl-Broadfield Plantation and other plantations, the communities of the Golden Isles, shrimp fleets at Darien, plus Brunswick and other small towns. The coast provides wildlife watching and birding in the marshes, live oak, palmetto hammocks, and the tidewater rivers and swamps.

Location: Southeast Georgia coast.

Drive route numbers: U.S. Highway 17, Georgia Highway 99, and several county sideroads leading to points of interest.

Travel season: This year-round drive is best traveled in the cooler months to avoid some of the bothersome biting insects such as gnats and mosquitoes.

Camping: Tent and trailer camping is available at Skidaway State Park south of Savannah. There is camping by reservation on Cumberland Island National Sea Shore, reachable only by commercial ferry or private boat.

Services: Lodging and food is available all along the drive. This is especially true in the Golden Isles area near Brunswick and Darien.

Nearby attractions: Savannah's historic section; Fort Stewart Military Reservation and Military Museum; Cumberland Island National Seashore; Kingsland, Saint Marys, and the nearby Kings Bay Submarine Base; Okefenokee Swamp and National Wildlife Refuge; fishing in the Satilla and Altamaha rivers, in the saltwater tidal streams, and on the islands' oceanside beaches.

The drive

For the most part, this drive follows US 17 along the Georgia coast from Midway to Jekyll Island. This federal highway has been replaced as a major north-south artery by Interstate 95, which leaves the older road open for more leisurely travel.

This is a route overflowing with history, beauty, and recreational opportunities. The earliest known residents were Guale (pronounced "wally") Indians who lived in villages on the coast and barrier islands.

The first European contact here was in 1562, when the French arrived on Jekyll Island. Four years later came Spanish soldiers and missionaries, followed by English traders. Warfare between these three nations continued until the British established control at the Battle of Bloody Marsh in 1742. This region has been battleground, playground, plantation land, and home to generations of people earning a living on the shore and from the sea.

Forests of pine, palmetto, and live oaks give way to coastal marshes washed daily by the tides. At one time, the entire eastern seaboard was covered by tidal grasslands such as these, but in most other places development and pollution have largely destroyed them. Due to efforts by conservation groups during the 1970s, Georgia now has the most extensive range of marshes still existing.

Commercial harvest of shrimp and crabs depends on the marshlands' ability to act as a nursery for sea creatures. Anglers here find sport in the winding waterways, seeking speckled seatrout and sheepshead, or fishing offshore for mackerel, bluefish, snapper, and tarpon.

Beaches on Saint Simon and Jekyll Islands lure vacationing families. These two barrier islands are heavily developed, with golf courses, resorts, homes, and shops. Farther north, Ossabaw, Sapelo, and Blackbeard islands are havens for wildlife and accessible only by boat.

On the shore, Harris Neck National Wildlife Refuge is an easy drive from US 17. This World War II-era airfield is now sanctuary and breeding ground for a multitude of animals and birds, including the endangered wood stork.

The drive begins in Midway on US 17, north of the intersection with U.S. Highway 84. Midway was settled in the mid-eighteenth century by Scotch Calvinists who built the Midway Church in 1792. The church has never been modernized, and the adjacent cemetery has graves dating prior to the church.

Midway counts among its past inhabitants the fathers of Oliver Wendell Holmes and Samuel F. B. Morse, as well as two of the three Georgians who signed the Declaration of Independence, Lyman Hall and Button Gwinnett. Midway calls itself "The Cradle of Revolutionary Spirit in Georgia." In fact, this county is named Liberty because the local patriots were so avid in their wish for independence that they sent representatives to the Continental Congress before the other Georgia colonists decided to do so. Midway Museum is a reproduction of a raised cottage-style house across from the church. It features furnishings, documents, and artifacts from the early 1700s to the late 1800s. Just south of the museum is a sign pointing to Sunbury Town and Fort Morris. It is 11 miles to this State Historic Site via Georgia Highway 38, where visitors will find what are said to be the only revolutionary war fortifications on the East Coast. The earth fort, Fort Morris, was active during the American Revolution; later, as Fort Defiance, it was active during the War of 1812. There is a small museum here, as well as walking trails leading around the fort and to the site of Sunbury, which at one time rivaled Savannah as a seaport.

About 5 miles south of Midway on US 17 you will come upon a sign indicating the Interstate Paper Company is near. If the wind is from the right direction you do not really need the sign. Your nose will tell you.

Abandoned buildings along the road once held motels, restaurants, and shops serving tourists when this was the main drag. When the interstate highway was completed in the 1970s, many of the businesses along US 17 closed or moved to the freeway exits. You come to one of these exits when the interstate highway crosses over US 17. A mile later a sign on the left identifies "The Smallest Church in America." A local woman, Agnes Harper, had the church built in 1950. Called Memory Chapel, the building measures 8'x10', and holds a dozen people including the preacher. It is open daily and there is a guest book inside where travelers have stopped and written comments about the church and their meditations there. Just past Memory Chapel, Georgia Highway 131 goes left 8 miles to Harris Neck National Wildlife Refuge. An army airfield during World War II, it is now home to a large population of animals, including every species of wading bird common to coastal Georgia, and includes breeding grounds for the endangered wood stork. The refuge has fishing piers, boat ramp, and a 4-mile designated auto route, much of it along the old runways and taxiways of the abandoned airstation.

At Eulonia, 8 miles farther down US 17, turn left on Georgia Highway 99. This narrow, two-lane road winds through the small communities of Crescent, Valona, Meridian, Carnigan, and Ridgeville before returning to US 17 at Darien. These towns sit along serpentine creeks running through the coastal marshes. Many of the residents earn their livings fishing and shrimping in the marsh and on the ocean beyond. The road is bordered with moss-draped live oaks, and its meandering course is a break from US 17, which tends to be arrow-straight, pine tree lined, and monotonous. Nine miles from your turn onto GA 99, a sign on the left points to the Sapelo

Island Marine Research Institute. A toll ferry serves the island, where a limited number of visitors can tour the research station, see Thomas Spalding's antebellum mansion, and visit the beaches, marsh ecosystems, and Hog Hammock. The residents of Hog Hammock community are directly descended from slaves who worked Sapelo Island's plantations. There is also a restricted amount of primitive camping available on the island, which is now known as Sapelo Island Estuarine Research Reserve. The station is operated by the University of Georgia. Reservations for the ferry are available in Darien at the Welcome Center on US 17.

Ridgeville, just outside Darien, is a residential community started at the turn of the century by prosperous timber merchants. It features a number of well-maintained Victorian-style homes set among the large live oak trees. The road here actually curves to accommodate the trees, winding among them.

Darien is Georgia's second oldest city after Savannah, founded in 1736 by Scotch Highlanders under Georgia's founder General James Oglethorpe as an outpost against Spanish attacks from Florida. Older still is the Fort King George Historic Site just east of Darien. This strongpoint was built in 1721, eleven years before the colony of Georgia was established.

From the early 1700s to the 1930s, Darien was a center of timber production. Logging crews cleared huge stands of gum and bald cypress from the river swamps and brought the logs here to be sawn into timber. Today it is home to a bustling fleet of shrimp boats, which you can see as you turn left and cross the bridge over the Darien River. Each spring the shrimp boats, painted, polished, and decorated, file under the bridge to receive a benediction and prayers for good fishing and safety in the annual Blessing of the Fleet. From the elevation of the bridge, you get a good vista of the salt marshes stretching east toward the Atlantic Ocean. At one time, marshes such as these bordered almost the entire Atlantic coastline of the United States, but development and pollution have taken most of them away. A nursery to many of the ocean's creatures, Georgia's marshes, now largely protected, are the most extensive on the eastern seaboard.

To the right is Butler's Island. Now the check station of the 27,000-acre Altamaha Wildlife Management Area (WMA), it was headquarters to extensive rice fields dating to 1788. Many of the dikes of the old plantation are still used to form ponds for overwintering waterfowl. The WMA provides hiking, fishing, spectacular coastal birding, and primitive camping in addition to hunting for deer, wild turkeys, hogs, and of course, ducks, geese, rail, snipe, and other game birds.

Four miles south of Darien, the Altamaha River spreads itself into several channels as it nears the ocean. This is the largest river flowing entirely in Georgia. Together with its major feeder streams, the Oconee and Ocmulgee, it travels more than 400 miles from its headwaters, draining more than 14,000

Live oaks line road along US 17 near Darien.

square miles of the central Piedmont and Coastal Plain. A mile past the Altamaha bridge is the entrance to Hofwyl-Broadfield Plantation Historic Site. From 1807 to 1973, one family owned this plantation, growing rice before the Civil War when slaves worked the fields and operating most recently as a dairy farm. The plantation fields, houses, and outbuildings are now preserved and administered by the Georgia Department of Natural Resources.

The road widens and traffic picks up as you enter Brunswick. This port city bills itself as "The Shrimp Capital of the World." During the warm months of the shrimping season, shrimp boats with shrouds of nets bring their catch to docks on the Brunswick River at Bay Street. This city is also an important shipping center, with container ships arriving from all parts of the world. During World War II, the Brunswick Ship Yard produced Liberty Ships. A model of one of these 447-foot-long freighters is in front of the Welcome Center at the intersection of US 17 with Saint Simons Causeway. The causeway leads to Saint Simons and Sea Islands and their multitude of attractions, including beaches, golf courses, and Fort Frederica National Monument. Saint Simons is the most developed of all Georgia's barrier islands with a full compliment of shopping, dining, and entertainment venues.

US 17 skirts the marshes past boat docks and marinas and spans the Brunswick River just south of town on Sidney Lanier Bridge.

A mile past the bridge, turn left on Georgia Highway 520, which leads 6 miles to Jekyll Island. Operated by a state authority, Jekyll Island was once the playground of the Pulitzers, Rockefellers, Morgans, and others of America's wealthiest families, many of whom built luxurious "cottages" on the island. These homes are now part of the Jekyll Island Club Historic District, and tours are available. There are also miles of beaches, hiking and bicycling trails, golf courses, and fishing available on the island, as well as camping and tourist accommodations. To return to I-95, go back to US 17 and continue south 6 miles. Kingsland, Saint Mary's, and Cumberland Island National Seashore are just north of the Florida border. The Okefenokee Swamp (see Drive 28) is 35 miles west of Kingsland via Georgia Highway 40.

Appendix
Sources of more Information
For more information on lands and events, please
contact the following agencies and organizations.

Drive 1

Cloudland Canyon State Park
Route 2, Box 150
Rising Fawn, GA 30738
(706) 657-4050

USDA Forest Service
Armuchee Ranger District
806 East Villanow Street
P.O. Box 465
LaFayette, GA 30728
(706) 638-1085

Drive 2

Superintendent
Chickamauga and Chattanooga
  National Military Park
P.O. Box 2128
Fort Oglethorpe, GA 30742
(706) 866-2512

Dalton Convention and
  Visitors Bureau
2211 Dug Gap Battle Road
Dalton, GA 30720
(706) 272-7676

Drive 3

USDA Forest Service
Armuchee Ranger District
806 East Villanow Street
P.O. Box 465
LaFayette, GA 30728
(706) 638-1085

Berry College
2277 Martha Berry Highway
Rome, GA 30165-9908
(800) 237-7942

Greater Rome Convention
  and Visitors Bureau
402 Civic Center Hill
P.O. Box 5823
Rome, GA 30162
(706) 295-5576

Regional Supervisor
Wildlife Resources Division
2592 Floyd Springs Road
Armuchee, GA 30105
(706) 295-6041

Drive 4

Chattooga County Chamber
  of Commerce
4 College Street
P.O. Box 217
Summerville, GA 30747
(706) 875-4033

Polk County Chamber
  of Commerce
604 Goodyear Street
Rockmart, GA 30153
(770) 684-8774

Drive 5

Cartersville–Bartow
  County Tourism Council
16 West Main Street
Cartersville, GA 30120
(770) 387-1357

Gordon County Chamber
of Commerce
300 South Wall Street
Calhoun, GA 30701
(706) 625-3200

Etowah Indian Mounds
State Historic Site
813 Indian Mounds Road SW
Cartersville, GA 30120
(770) 387-3747

New Echota State
Historic Site
1211 Chatsworth Highway NE
Calhoun, GA 30701
(706) 629-8151

Greater Rome Convention
and Visitor Bureau
402 Civic Center Hill
P.O. Box 5823
Rome, GA 30126
(706) 295-5576

Drive 6

USDA Forest Service
Cohutta Ranger District
401 Old Ellijay Road
Chatsworth, GA 30705
(706) 695-6736

Fort Mountain State Park
181 Fort Mountain Road
Chatsworth, GA 30705
(706) 695-2621

Chatsworth–Murry County
Chamber of Commerce
120 West Fort Street # 104
P.O. Box 327
Chatsworth, GA 30705
(706) 695-6060

Drive 7

Georgia Marble Works
(770) 692-5600

Amicalola Falls State
Park and Lodge
Star Route
Dawsonville, GA 30534
(706) 265-2885

Pickens County Chamber
of Commerce
263 Main Street
P.O. Box 327
Jasper, GA 30143
(706) 692-5600

Gilmer County Chamber
of Commerce
P.O. Box 818
Ellijay, GA 30540
(706) 635-7400

Drive 8

Gilmer County Chamber
of Commerce
P.O. Box 818
Ellijay, GA 30540
(706) 635-7400

U.S. Army Corps of Engineers
Carters Lake
P.O. Box 96
Oakman, GA 30732-0096
(706) 334-2248

Carters Lake Marina & Resort
Route 4, Box 41503
Chatsworth, GA 30705
(706) 276-4891

Chatsworth–Murray County
Chamber of Commerce
120 W. Fort St. #104
P.O. Box 327
Chatsworth, GA 30705
(706) 695-6060

Drive 9

USDA Forest Service
Chestatee Ranger District
1015 Tipton Drive
Dahlonega, GA 30533
(706) 864-6173

USDA Forest Service
Brasstown Ranger District
U.S. Highway 19/129 South
P.O. Box 9
Blairsville, GA 30512
(706) 745-6928

Vogel State Park
Route 1, Box 1230
Blairsville, GA 30512
(706) 745-2628

Dahlonega Chamber
of Commerce
101 South Park Street
Dahlonega, GA 30533
(706) 864-3711

White County Chamber
of Commerce
1700 North Main Street #A
Cleveland, GA 30528
(706) 865-5356

Drive 10

Greater Helen Area Chamber
of Commerce/Festhalle
Edelweiss Street
Helen, GA 30545
(706) 878-3677

Towns County Chamber
of Commerce
U.S. Highway 76
The Hamlet, #4
Hiawassee, GA 30546
(706) 896-4966

Blairsville–Union County
Chamber of Commerce
385 Blue Ridge Highway
Blairsville, GA 30512
(706) 745-5789

Unicoi State Park and Lodge
P.O. Box 1029
Helen, GA 30545
(706) 878-2201

Dukes Creek/Smithgall
Woods Conservation Area
61 Tsalaki Trail
Helen, GA 30545
(706) 878-3087

USDA Forest Service
Chattooga Ranger District
Burton Road
P.O. Box 196
Clarksville, GA 30523
(706) 754-6221

USDA Forest Service
Brasstown Ranger District
1881 Highway 515
P.O. Box 465
Blairsville, GA 30512
(706) 745-6928

Drive 11

Tallulah Gorge State Park
P.O. Box 248
Tallulah Falls, GA 30573
(706) 754-8257

Terrora Park and Campground
Tallulah Falls, GA 30573
(706) 754-6036

Habersham County Chamber
  of Commerce
P.O. Box 366
Cornelia, GA 30531
(706) 778-4654

USDA Forest Service
Tallulah Ranger District
825 Highway 441 South
P.O. Box 438
Clayton, GA 30525
(706) 782-3320

USDA Forest Service
Chattooga Ranger District
Highway 197 North Burton Road
P.O. Box 196
Clarkesville, GA 30523
(706) 754-6221

Drive 12

Rabun County Chamber
  of Commerce
P.O. Box 761
Clayton, GA 30525
(706) 782-4812

USDA Forest Service
Tallulah Ranger District
825 Highway 441 South
P.O. Box 438
Clayton, GA 30525
(706) 782-3320

Black Rock Mountain State Park
Mountain City, GA 30562
(706) 746-2141

Drive 13

Toccoa and Stephens County
  Welcome Center
Traveler's Rest State Historic Site
Route 3
Toccoa, GA 30577
(706) 886-2256

USDA Forest Service
Chattooga Ranger District
Highway 197 North Burton Drive
P.O. Box 196
Clarksville, GA 30523
(706) 754-6221

Drive 14

Elbert County Chamber
  of Commerce
148 College Avenue
Elberton, GA 30635
(706) 283-5651

Hart County Chamber
  of Commerce
P.O. Box 793
31 S. Howell St.
Hartwell, GA 30653
(706) 376-8590

Hart State Park
1515 Hart Park Road
Hartwell, GA 30463
(706) 376-8756

Victoria Bryant State Park
and Golf Course
Route 1, Box 1767
Royston, GA 30662
(706) 245-6270

Drive 15

Hard Labor Creek State Park
P.O. Box 247
Rutledge, GA 30663
(770) 557-2863

A. H. Stephens State Historic Park
P.O. Box 235
Crawfordville, GA 30631
(706) 456-2602

Covington–Newton County
Chamber of Commerce
2100 Washington Street
Covington, GA 30209
(770) 787-3868

Madison–Morgan Chamber
of Commerce
115 East Jefferson Street
Madison, GA 30650
(706) 342-4454

Green County Chamber
of Commerce
112 South Main Street
Greensboro, GA 30642
(706) 453-7592

Drive 16

Augusta–Richmond County
Convention and Visitors Bureau
32 Eighth Street, Suite 200
Augusta, GA 30901
(706) 823-6600

Lincolnton–Lincoln County
Chamber of Commerce
P.O. Box 810
Lincolnton, GA 30817
(706) 359-7970

Washington–Wilkes County
Chamber of Commerce
104 East Liberty Street
P.O. Box 661
Washington, GA 30673
(706) 678-2013

Mistletoe State Park
Route 1, Box 335,
Appling, GA 30802
(706) 541-0321

Elijah Clark State Park
Box 293, Route 4
Lincolnton, GA 30817
(706) 359-3458

U.S. Army Corps of Engineers
P.O. Box 889
Savannah, GA 31402-0889
(912) 652-5997

Drive 17

Newton County Chamber
of Commerce
2100 Washington Street
Covington, GA 30209
(770) 787-3868

Milledgeville–Baldwin
  Tourism & Trade
200 West Hancock Street
P.O. Box 219
Milledgeville, GA 31061
(912) 452-4687

Oconee National Forest
Oconee Ranger District
349 Forsyth Street
Monticello, GA 31064
(706) 468-2244

Panola Mountain State Park
2600 Highway 155 SW
Stockbridge, GA 30281
(770) 389-7801

Drive 18

High Falls State Park
Route 5, Box 202-A
Jackson, GA 30233
(770) 994-5080

Indian Springs State Park
P.O. Box 3969
Jackson, GA 30334
(770) 775-7241

Jarrell Plantation State Historic Site
Route 1, Box 220
Juliette, GA 31064
(912) 986-5172

Oconee National Forest
Oconee Ranger District
349 Forsyth Street
Monticello, GA 31064
(706) 468-2244

U.S. Fish and Wildlife Service
Piedmont National Wildlife Refuge
Route 1, Box 670
Round Oak, GA 31038
(912) 986-5441

Butts County Chamber of Commerce
143 East College Street
P.O. Box 147
Jackson, GA 30233
(770) 775-4839

Drive 19

Macon I-16 Welcome Center
200 Cherry Street
Macon, GA 31201
(912) 743-3401

Ocmulgee National Monument
National Park Service
1207 Emery Highway
Macon, GA 31201
(912) 752-8257

Kaolin Festival
P.O. Box 582
Sandersville, GA 30820
(912) 552-3288

Drive 20

Pine Mountain Tourism Association
P.O. Box 177
Pine Mountain, GA 31822
(706) 663-4000 or (800) 441-3502

Meriwether County Chamber
  of Commerce
P.O. Box 9
Federal Building
Warm Springs, GA 31830
(706) 655-2558

Drive 21

Thomaston–Upson County
  Chamber of Commerce
201 South Center Street
Thomaston, GA 30286
(706) 647-9686

Drive 22

Columbus Chamber of Commerce
Convention and Visitors Bureau
801 Front Avenue
P.O. Box 2768
Columbus, GA 31902
(706) 322-1613 or (800) 999-1613

Providence Canyon State Park
Route 1, Box 158
Lumpkin, GA 31815
(912) 838-6202

Florence Marina State Park
Route 1, Box 36
Omaha, GA 31821
(912) 838-4244

Drive 23

Bainbridge–Decatur County
  Chamber of Commerce
P.O. Box 736
Bainbridge, GA 31717
(912) 246-4774

Kolomoki Mounds State
  Historic Park
Route1, Box 114
Blakely, GA 31723
(912) 723-5296

George T. Bagby State Park
  and Lodge
Route 1, Box 201
Fort Gaines, GA 31751
(912) 768-2571

Cotton Hill Park
U.S. Army Corps of Engineers
Fort Gaines, GA 31751
(912) 768-3061

Seminole State Park
Route 2
Donalsonville, GA 31754
(912) 861-3137

Florence Marina State Park
Route 1, Box 36
Omaha, GA 31821
(912) 838-4244

Drive 24

Peach County Chamber of Commerce
114 Vineville Street
Fort Valley, GA 31030
(912) 825-3733

Andersonville Welcome Center
114 Church Street
Andersonville, GA 31711
(912) 924-2558

Americus–Sumter County
  Chamber of Commerce
400 West Lamar Street
P.O. Box 724
Americus, GA 31709
(912) 924-2646

Plains Tour Service
P.O. Box 346
Plains, GA 31780
(912) 824-7740

Massee Lane Gardens/Museum
One Massee Lane
Fort Valley, GA 31030
(912)967-2358

Jimmy Carter National Historic Site
Route 1, Box 800
Plains, GA 31709
(912)824-3413

Georgia Visitor Information Center
U.S. Highway 280
Plains, GA 31780
(912)824-7477

Drive 25

Hawkinsville–Pulaski
  Chamber of Commerce
100 Lumpkin Street
P.O. Box 447
Hawkinsville, GA 31036
(912)783-1717

Hazlehurst–Jeff Davis County
  Chamber of Commerce
507 East Jarman Street
P.O. Box 536
Hazlehurst, GA 31539
(912)375-4543

Georgia Wildlife Resources Division
Game Management Office
Fitzgerald, GA
(912) 423-2988

Little Ocmulgee State Park
P.O. Box 97
McRae, GA 31055
(912) 868-2832

General Coffee State Park
Route 2, Box 83
Nicholls, GA 31554
(912) 384-7082

Drive 26

Claxton Local Welcome Center
4 North Duval Street
U.S. Highway 301
Claxton, GA 30417
(912) 739-2281

Vidalia Tourism Council
2805 Lyons Highway
Vidalia, GA 30474
(912) 537-7387

Little Ocmulgee State Park
P.O. Box 97
McRae, GA 31055
(912) 868-2832

Gordonia–Alatamaha State Park
P.O. Box 1047
Reidsville, GA 30453
(912) 557-6444

Drive 27

Valdosta–Lowndes County
  Chamber of Commerce
416 North Ashley Street
Valdosta, GA 31601
(912) 247-8100

Valdosta–Lowndes County
  Convention and Visitors Bureau
1703 Norman Drive, Suite F
Valdosta, GA 31602
(912) 245-0513

Destination Thomasville
  Tourism Authority
P.O. Box 1540
Thomasville, GA 31799
(912) 225-5222

Area Manager
Grand Bay Wildlife
  Management Area
Route 1, Box 316
Lakeland, GA 31635

Okefenokee National Wildlife
  Refuge (For Banks Lake National
  Wildlife Refuge)
U.S. Fish and Wildlife Service
Route 2, Box 338
Folkston, GA 31537
(912) 496-3331

Drive 28

Refuge Manager
U.S. Fish and Wildlife Service
Okefenokee National Wildlife Refuge
Route 2, Box 338
Folkston, GA 31537
(912) 496-3331

Stephen C. Foster State Park
Fargo, GA 31631
(912) 637-5274

Okefenokee Swamp Park
Waycross, GA 31501
(912) 283-0583

Laura S. Walker State Park
5653 Laura S. Walker Road
Waycross, GA 31501
(912) 287-4900

Waycross-Ware Tourism Bureau
200 Lee Avenue
P.O. Box 137
Waycross, GA 31502
(912) 283-3742

Drive 29

McIntosh County Chamber of
  Commerce and Welcome Center
Fort King George Drive
Highway 17
Darien, GA 31305
(912) 437-4192 or (912) 437-6684

Brunswick-Golden Isles Visitors
Bureau
4 Glynn Avenue
Brunswick, GA 31520
(912) 265-0620 or
(800) 933-COAST

Georgia Visitor Information
  Center at Kingsland/St. Marys
I-95
Kingsland, GA 31548
(912) 729-3253

Hofwyl–Broadfield Plantation
  State Historic Site
Route 10, Box 83
Brunswick, GA 31520
(912) 264-9263

Skidaway Island State Park
Savannah, GA 31406
(912) 356-2523

About the Authors

Donald W. Pfitzer knows the Georgia outdoors. Recently retired, Don spent thirty-three years with the U. S. Fish and Wildlife Service as a biologist and public affairs officer. Don is a member and past president of the Southeastern Outdoor Press Association and the Georgia Outdoor Writers Association. He is also a member of the Outdoor Writers Association of America, charter member of the Georgia Conservancy, and a member of other conservation organizations. Don continues to be active in environmental education, writing, and photography. This is his second book.

LeRoy Powell is an award-winning television reporter and commentator. His travel specials have been seen on the Arts and Entertainment network and Georgia Public Television. He is also an essayist for MotoWorld network on ESPN and contributor to outdoor magazines. He is a graduate of the University of Georgia. He lives in Lithonia, Georgia, with his wife and two children. This is his second book.